It's Code Red!

Cartoons from *Mail & Guardian*, *Sunday Times* and *The Times*

JACANA

Acknowledgements: A big thank you to Mike Wills for writing the captions and deftly adapting to my idiosyncratic style; thanks to my editors at the Mail & Guardian *(Angela Quintal, Chris Roper), at the* Sunday Times *(Phylicia Oppelt) and at* The Times *(Stephen Haw) and their production staff; my website, ePublications and rights Manager Richard Hainebach; my assistant Eleanora Bresler; Roberto for colouring the cartoons on pp. 3, 33 and 68; Bridget Impey, Russell Martin and all at Jacana; Claudine Willatt-Bate; Nomalizo Ndlazi; and my family: Karina, Tevya and Nina.*

10 Orange Street
Sunnyside
Auckland Park 2092
South Africa
(+27 11) 628 3200
www.jacana.co.za

in association with

© Jonathan Shapiro, 2014

All rights reserved.

ISBN 978-1-4314-2099-5

Cover design by Jonathan Shapiro

Page layout by Claudine Willatt-Bate
Printed and bound by Creda Communications
Job no. 002364

See a complete list of Jacana titles at www.jacana.co.za

See Zapiro's list and archive at www.zapiro.com

One last time, for Madiba

ZAPIRO annuals
The Madiba Years (1996)
The Hole Truth (1997)
End of Part One (1998)
Call Mr Delivery (1999)
The Devil Made Me Do It! (2000)
The ANC Went in 4x4 (2001)
Bushwhacked (2002)
Dr Do-Little and the African Potato (2003)
Long Walk to Free Time (2004)
Is There a Spin Doctor In the House? (2005)
Da Zuma Code (2006)
Take Two Veg and Call Me In the Morning (2007)
Pirates of Polokwane (2008)
Don't Mess With the President's Head (2009)
Do You Know Who I Am?! (2010)
The Last Sushi (2011)
But Will It Stand Up In Court? (2012)
My Big Fat Gupta Wedding (2013)

Other books
The Mandela Files (2008)
VuvuzelaNation (2013)
Democrazy (2014)

The president tells a Limpopo evangelical congregation that God has made a connection between Government and the church and 'as a church you should pray for it'

10 October 2013

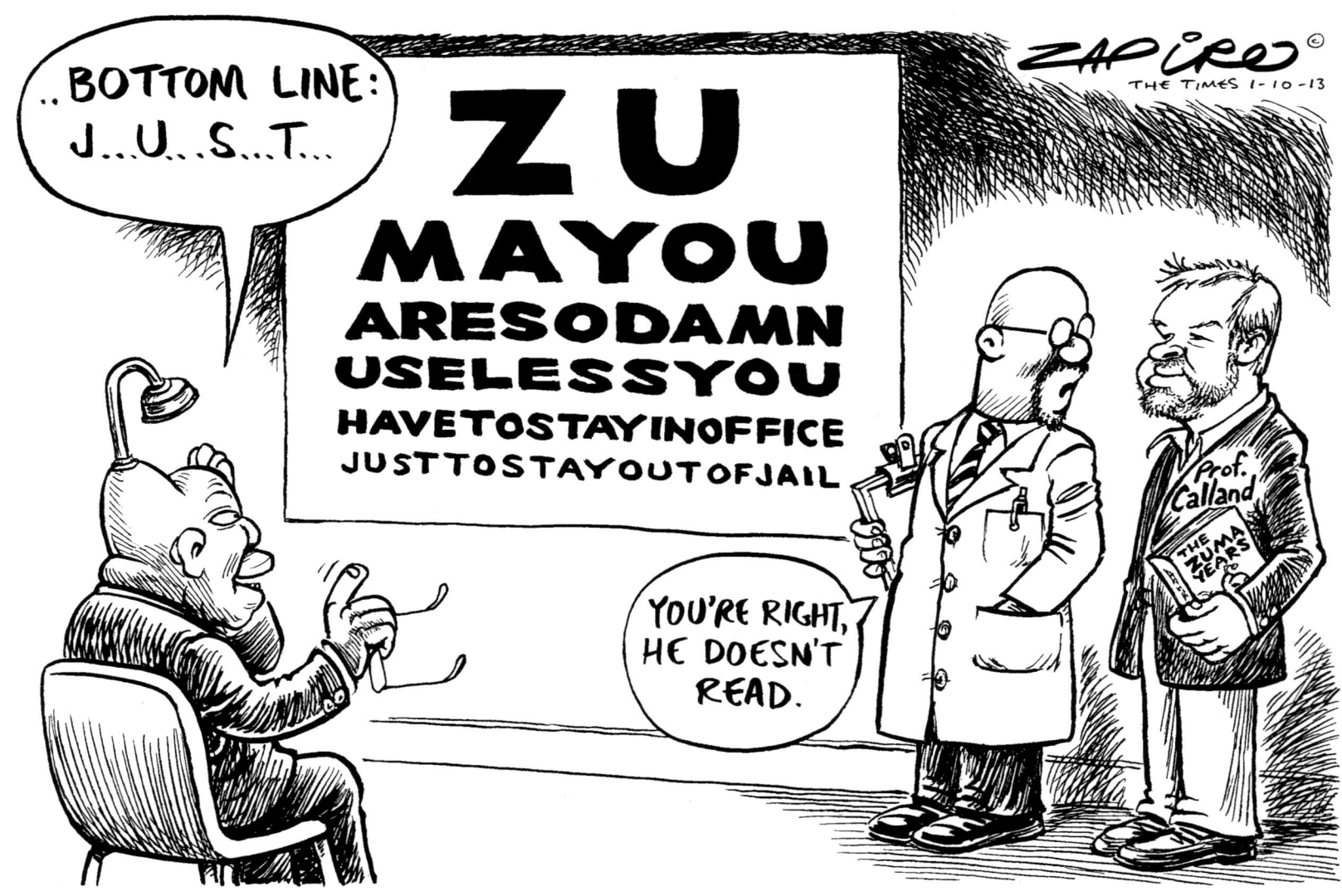

Leading political analyst causes a storm with a remark that our president doesn't read the right stuff for modern sophisticated government

1 October 2013

Lt-Col Christine Anderson is a fall gal in Guptagate. Her affidavit confirms what everyone knew – the president is 'Number One' named in a Justice Department report.

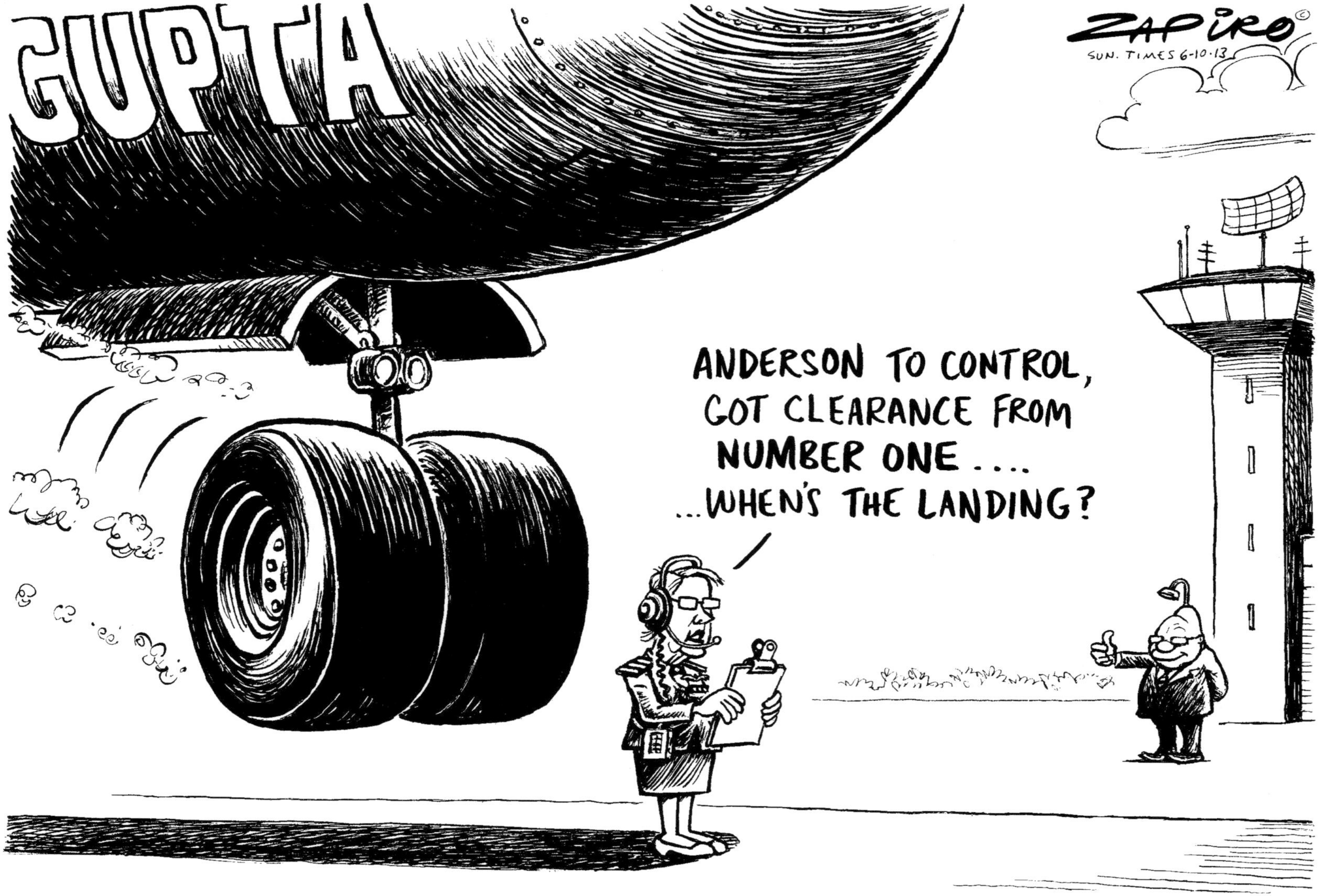
GUPTA
ZAPIRO©
SUN. TIMES 6-10-13
ANDERSON TO CONTROL, GOT CLEARANCE FROM NUMBER ONE.... ...WHEN'S THE LANDING?

6 October 2013

3 October 2013

New Northern Cape premier chows her way through taxpayers' money.
Her party says the media exposés are racist and sexist.

The same Constitutional Court judges who alleged judicial misconduct against Cape Judge President John Hlophe for interference in a case involving Zuma, launch legal moves to block the complaints being investigated

8 October 2013

10 October 2013

Manoeuvres within the AU to withdraw from the International Criminal Court because of claims that it's unfairly targeting African leaders for crimes against humanity

Latest estimates put costs of the presidential homestead 'security' upgrades at over R200m. The Public Works minister declares a task team report into the scandal 'classified'.

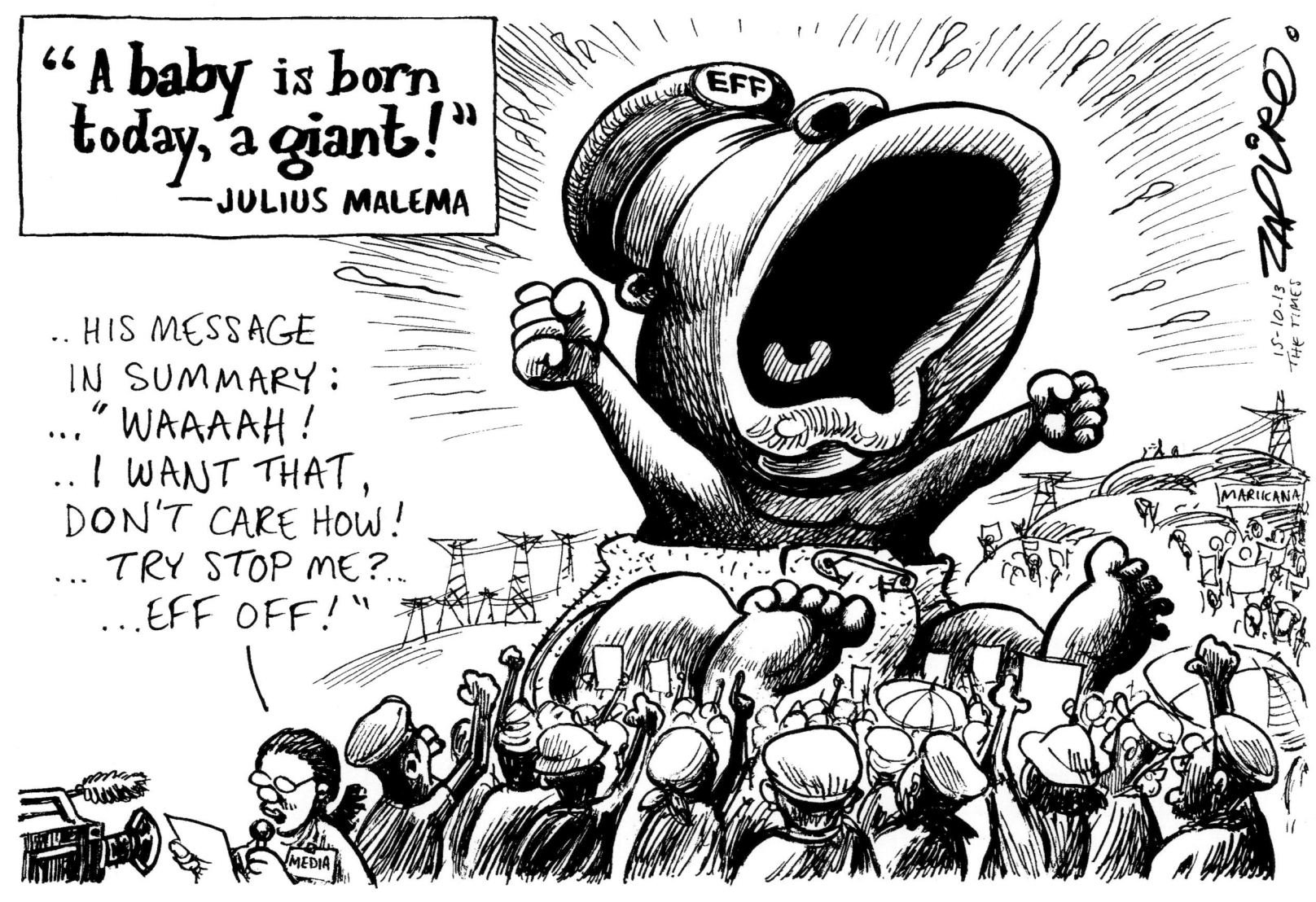

15 October 2013 Six months before the election the ANC Youth League renegade launches his very own party

24 October 2013

More fast-talking from Zuma's spin doctor Mac Maharaj after his boss undiplomatically disses Malawian roads

27 October 2013

The Indians use their financial muscle to bully SA administrators into sidelining their own CEO Haroon Lorgat for the duration of the tour to South Africa because of past personal grudges

31 October 2013

The national police commissioner completes a disastrous first year in office, which included the Marikana massacre

31 October 2013

And now it's alleged she defeated the ends of justice by warning a senior colleague that he was the subject of a Hawks' corruption probe

Nineteen years after they cooked up a mad plot to kill Nelson Mandela, five members of the right-wing 'bomb squad' get long sentences

3 November 2013

5 November 2013

The highly paid advocate who received R13m as his severance package after a destructive term as CEO of the SABC joins Julius in protest against the ANC's 'neo-liberal policies'

In Cairo one ailing former president remains on trial for complicity in the death of protesters while the military overthrows the democratically-elected Muslim Brotherhood government and puts its leader in the dock

7 November 2013

Government's latest way to stall the release of Madonsela's report on Nkandla spending is to interdict her for breaching state security

12 November 2013

10 November 2013 — Anant Singh's long-awaited biopic premieres in SA

The DA in parliament, headed by Lindiwe Mazibuko, supports black empowerment legislation. Party leader Helen Zille orders a backtrack sparking the ire of black members, a shadow cabinet reshuffle and confusion all round.

14 November 2013

17 November 2013

He has a dodgy history, is linked to underworld killings and his associates are being murdered. And he seems untouchable.

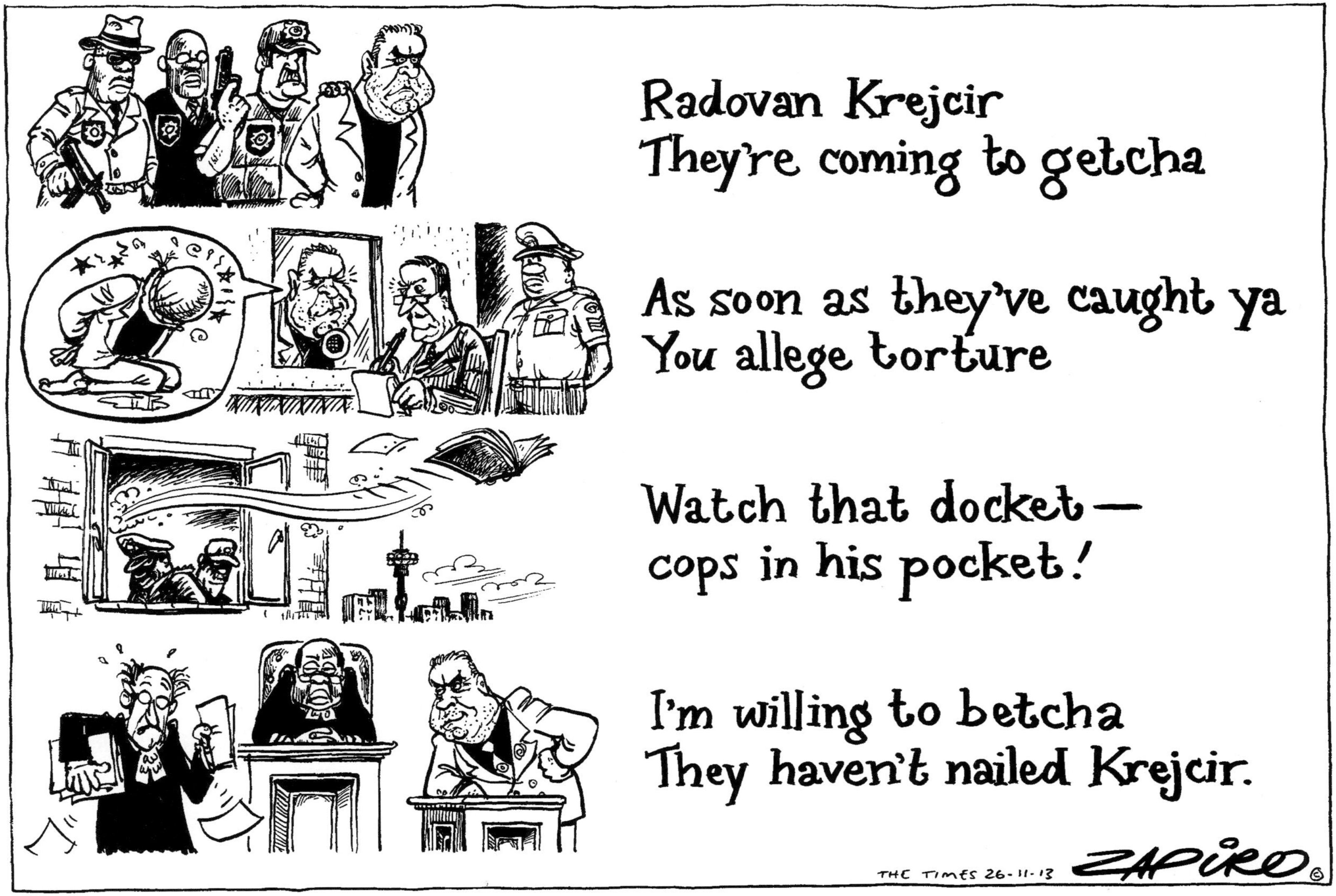
Radovan Krejcir
They're coming to getcha
As soon as they've caught ya
You allege torture
Watch that docket—
cops in his pocket!
I'm willing to betcha
They haven't nailed Krejcir.
THE TIMES 26-11-13
ZAPIRO ©

26 November 2013

Finally arrested on charges of attempted murder and kidnapping,
he claims he was beaten up by the cops

28 November 2013

US seals a landmark agreement with Tehran on its nuclear programme.
Benjamin Netanyahu is predictably outraged.

21 November 2013   The cabinet backs down at the last minute on its legal challenge against publication of her report

THE HOUSE THAT JACOB BUILT

SECURITY CLUSTER

THESE ARE THE STOOGES ALL PUFFED UP
WHO'LL NEVER ADMIT HOW THEY STUFFED UP
SPENDING MILLIONS OF TAXPAYERS' MONEY
AND THEN MAKING UP STORIES (HELLUVA FUNNY!)
DEFENDING EXTRAVAGANT BITS AND PIECES
FOR **JACOB** AND WIVES, KIDS, NEPHEWS AND NIECES.
RONDAWELS AND HOUSES OF VARYING SIZE
WERE PAID FOR BY JACOB (HMMM!..THIS SOUNDS LIKE LIES)
THE PUBLIC (THEY SAY) IS JUST FOOTING THE BILL
FOR **SECURITY FEATURES** — ONLY **200 MIL**!
THE FENCES AND GATES KEEP OUT '**LOCAL MARAUDERS**'
(WE WISH THEY HAD SAFEGUARDS AGAINST **TENDER FRAUDERS**)
FOR SECURITY GUARDS THERE ARE **TWO SOCCER PITCHES**
AND LASERS WITH BACKUP IN CASE THERE ARE GLITCHES
THERE'S PROTECTION FROM **EARTHQUAKES** (WHICH NEVER OCCUR)
AND DITTO FOR **FLOODS** ('COS IT'S BEST TO BE SURE!)
THERE ARE **TWO HELIPADS** AND ROADS THAT THEY'LL WIDEN
AND A **NEW CHICKEN COOP** THAT IS HARDER TO HIDE IN (!!)
THEY'VE SECURED JACOB'S SAFETY IN EVERY WHICH SECTOR
— EXCEPT **NOBODY'S** SAFE FROM THE **PUBLIC PROTECTOR**!

SO THIS IS THE HOUSE THAT **JACOB** BUILT
... AND SO DID **YOU** AND SO DID **I**
AND SO DID **SIPHO** AND **PENNY** AND **TY**
AND **VUYO** AND **HANIEF** AND **THANDI** AND **JULIE**
AND **FANIE** AND **MANNY** AND **ABDUL** AND **THULI**
THIS IS THE HOUSE THAT **ALL** OF US PAID FOR
BUT IT'S ONLY **JACOB** WHOM IT WAS MADE FOR!
..WHICH IS WHY YOU'RE IRATE THAT IF YOU TAKE A **PICTURE**
THOSE HIGH-HANDED STOOGES HAVE VOWED TO CONVICT YA!

A SELFIE AT NKANDLA? ..ME TOO!

24 November 2013

The Nkandla saga just gets weirder – two security ministers claim it's illegal for the media to take and publish images of the sprawling site

Cost of the swimming pool at Nkandla: R2.8m.
Oh, and it's officially a 'fire pool' for extinguishing any blazes on the thatched roofs.

ANC secretary general Gwede Mantashe calls for Madonsela to release her report urgently, suggesting she's the one delaying it as a political ploy ahead of the elections

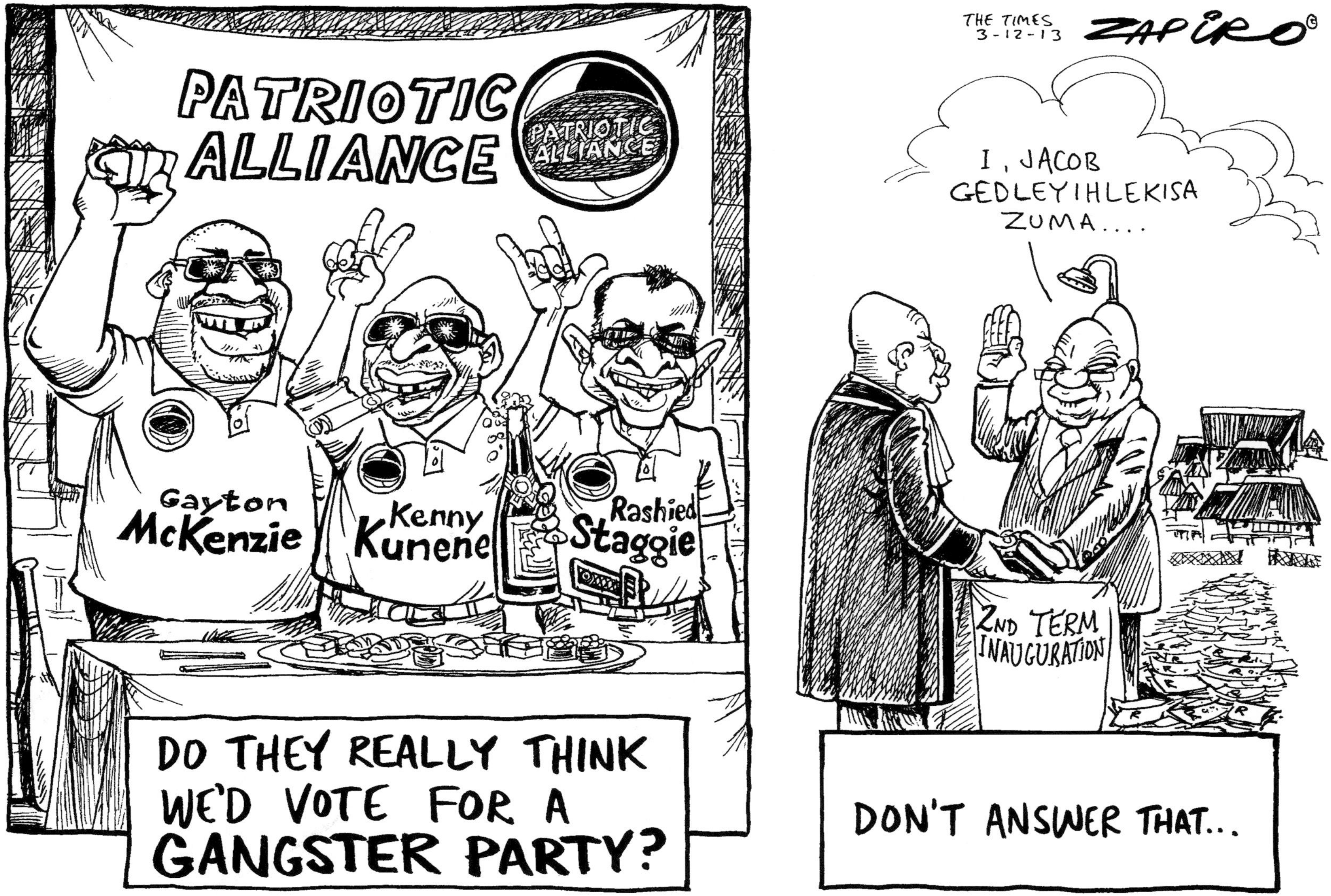
PATRIOTIC ALLIANCE
PATRIOTIC ALLIANCE
Gayton McKenzie
Kenny Kunene
Rashied Staggie
DO THEY REALLY THINK WE'D VOTE FOR A GANGSTER PARTY?
THE TIMES 3-12-13
ZAPIRO
I, JACOB GEDLEYIHLEKISA ZUMA....
2ND TERM INAUGURATION
DON'T ANSWER THAT...

3 December 2013 A nationwide collection of shady skelms band together to contest the election

6 December 2013 — Gauteng e-tolls go live. Cosatu declares Black Tuesday and slams 'power-drunk' cadres.

8 December 2013   5 December 2013 – the news the nation dreaded to hear

Two days later, four-times world champion and the shortest boxer ever to hold a title also passes on

10 December 2013

12 December 2013 — Public viewing at the Union Buildings

12 December 2013

Memorial service at Soccer City. One president is praised for soaring oratory, another cops a chorus of loud boos.

Media sensation over unqualified and unscreened interpreter for the deaf,
Thamsanqa Jantjie, and his incomprehensible hand gestures

15 December 2013

18 December 2013 — After his burial in Qunu a nine-metre-high statue of Madiba is unveiled by Zuma

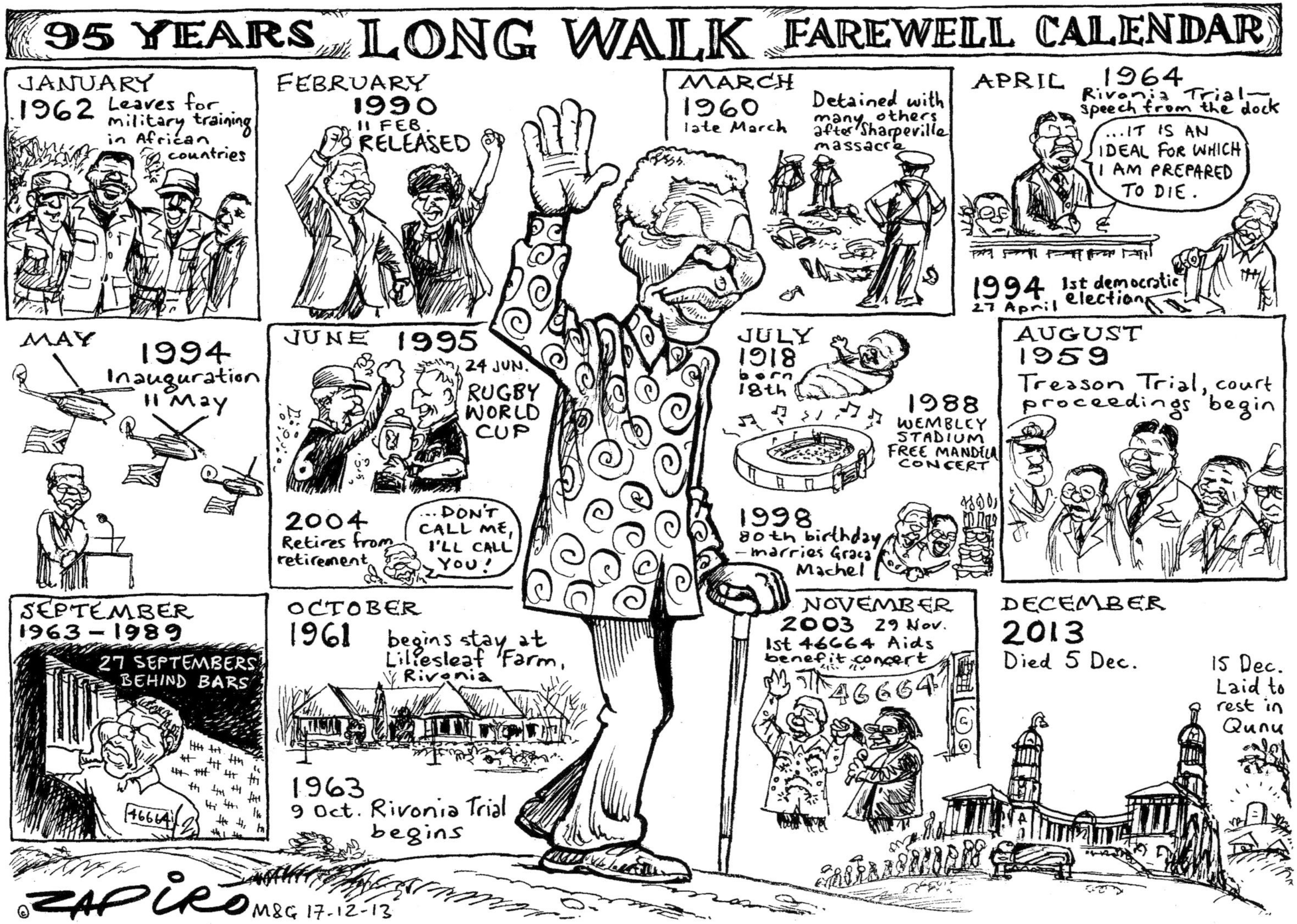
95 YEARS LONG WALK FAREWELL CALENDAR
JANUARY
1962 Leaves for military training in African countries
FEBRUARY
1990 11 FEB. RELEASED
MARCH
1960 late March
Detained with many others after Sharpeville massacre
APRIL 1964
Rivonia Trial— speech from the dock
...IT IS AN IDEAL FOR WHICH I AM PREPARED TO DIE.
1994 27 April 1st democratic election
MAY
1994 Inauguration 11 May
JUNE 1995
24 JUN. RUGBY WORLD CUP
2004 Retires from retirement
...DON'T CALL ME, I'LL CALL YOU!
JULY
1918 born 18th
1988 WEMBLEY STADIUM FREE MANDELA CONCERT
1998 80th birthday —marries Graça Machel
AUGUST
1959
Treason Trial, court proceedings begin
SEPTEMBER
1963–1989
27 SEPTEMBERS BEHIND BARS
46664
OCTOBER
1961 begins stay at Liliesleaf Farm, Rivonia
1963 9 Oct. Rivonia Trial begins
NOVEMBER
2003 29 Nov. 1st 46664 Aids benefit concert
46664
DECEMBER
2013 Died 5 Dec.
15 Dec. Laid to rest in Qunu
© ZAPIRO M&G 17-12-13

17 December 2013

Vain new media mogul can't make up his mind. Was *Cape Times* editor Alide Dasnois abruptly fired or merely re-deployed? And was it because of her paper's coverage of Mandela's death or the story on corruption allegations against his company Sekunjalo?

19 December 2013

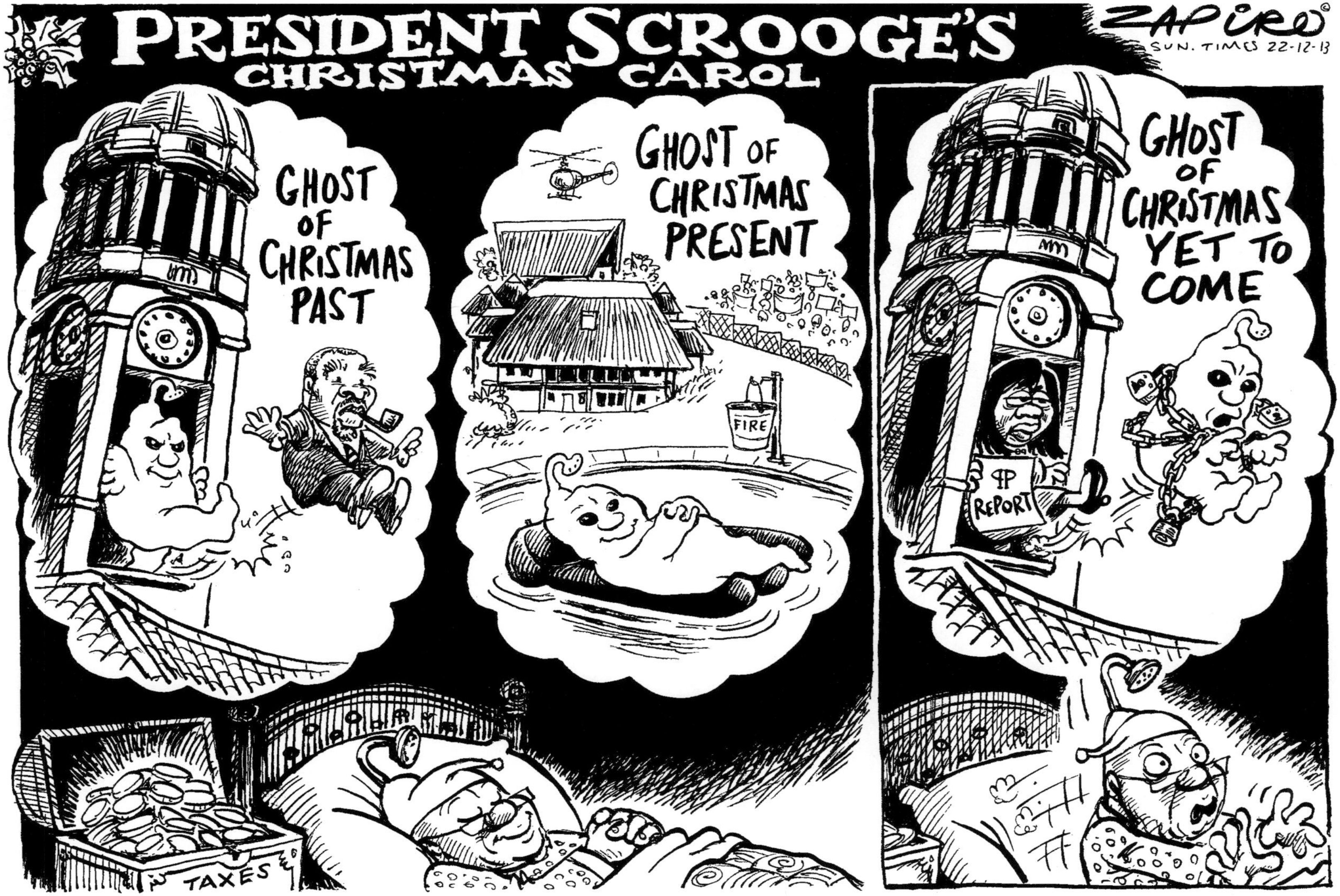
PRESIDENT SCROOGE'S CHRISTMAS CAROL
ZAPIRO©
SUN. TIMES 22-12-13
GHOST OF CHRISTMAS PAST
GHOST OF CHRISTMAS PRESENT
FIRE
GHOST OF CHRISTMAS YET TO COME
PP REPORT
TAXES

22 December 2013

14 January 2014 — The ruling party launches a predictable potage of promises 'to move South Africa forward'

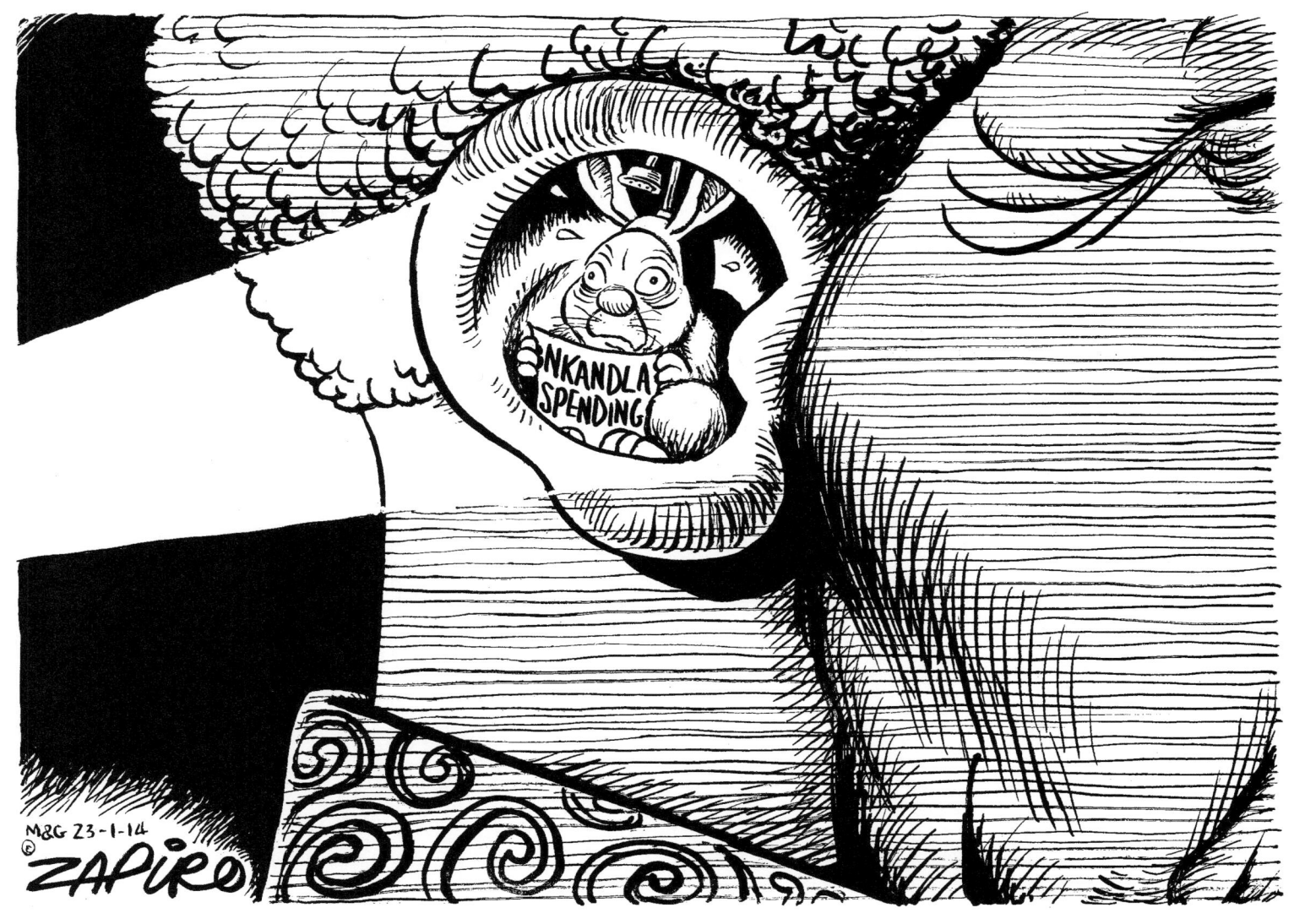

Forbidden from signing their new Madiba colossus, miffed sculptors hide a tiny bronze rabbit inside the statue's ear as a trademark

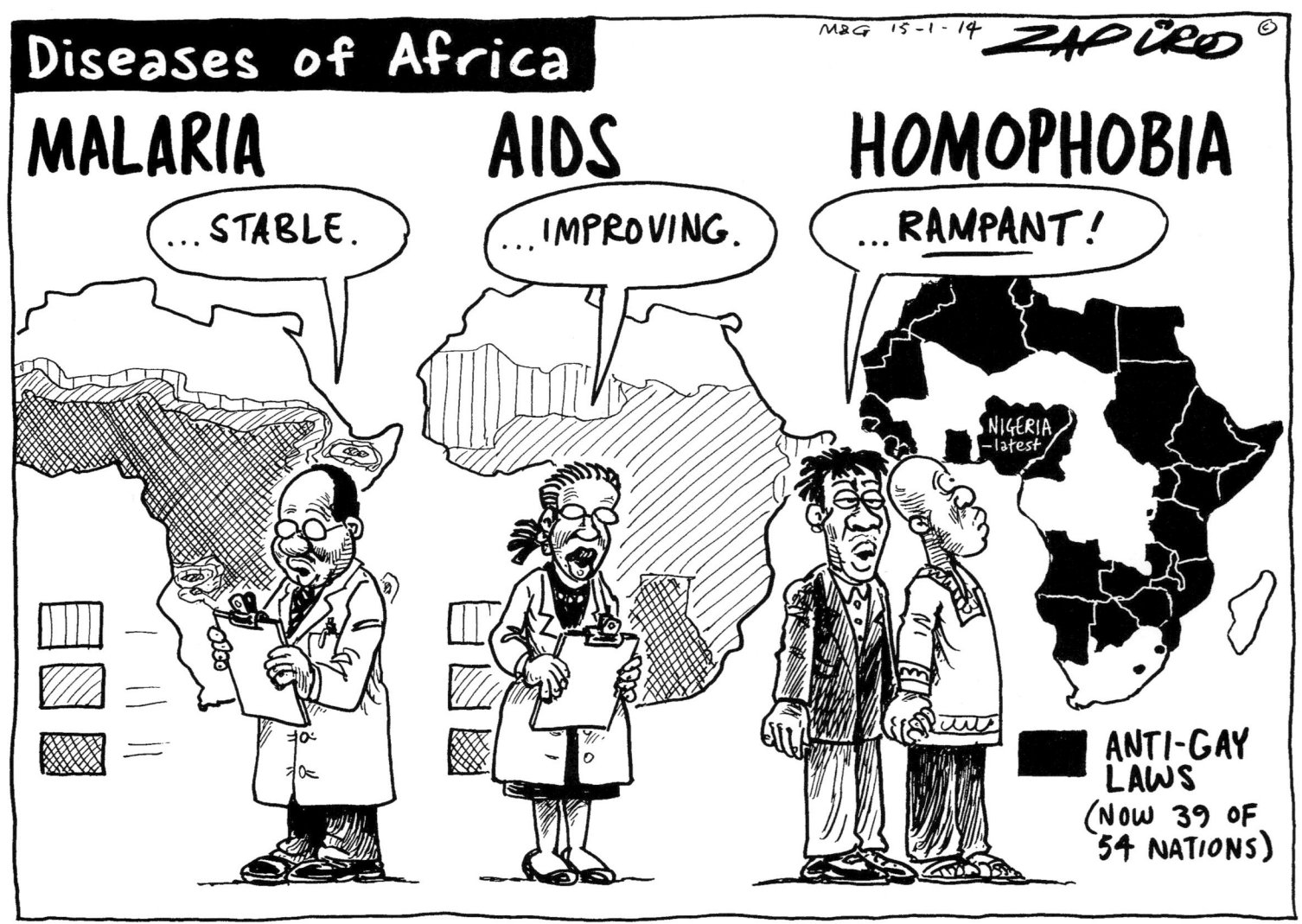

15 January 2014 — Nigeria bans same-sex relationships and criminalises homosexual organisations

23 January 2014   The tollroads' operator is under fire for sending out some wildly inaccurate accounts

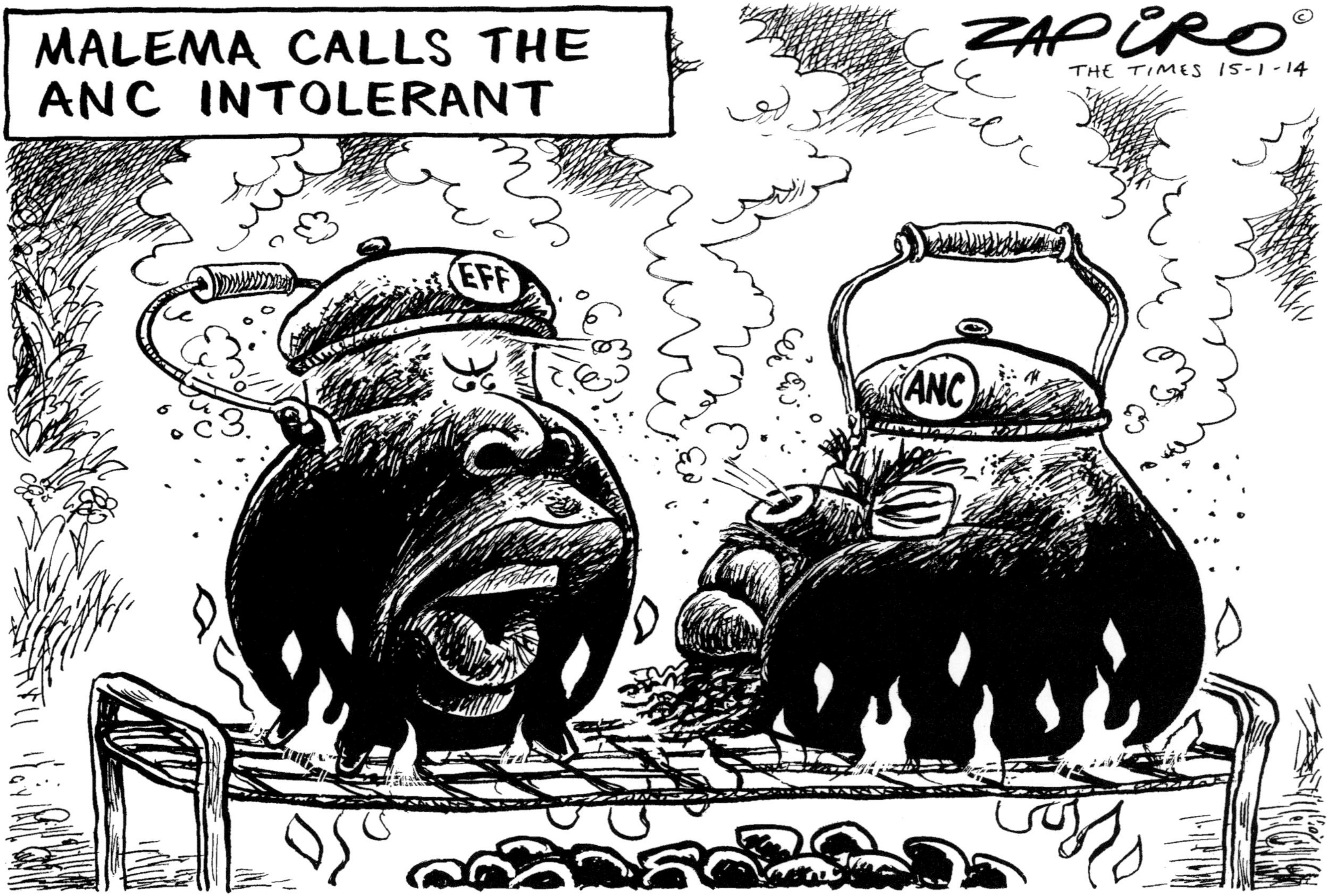
MALEMA CALLS THE ANC INTOLERANT
ZAPIRO ©
THE TIMES 15-1-14
EFF
ANC

15 January 2014

The young and the old of SA politics publicly reconcile after Julius had famously called Mangosuthu 'a factory fault' and been described as 'an ill-bred brat' in return

30 January 2014

29 January 2014

Zille thinks she has a 'game changer'. She dramatically reveals Agang's Mamphela Ramphele as the DA's presidential candidate

The new arrival right at the top of the party puts noses out of joint

4 February 2014 — The 'historic' deal unravels after only five days of political chaos and recrimination

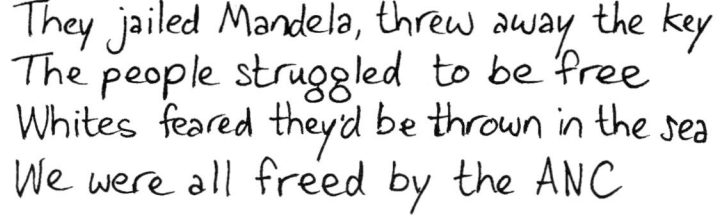

Born in a divided state
Torn apart by apartheid
Boere put a rifle in my hand
Told me to kill my fellow man

Born in the R.S.A., I was born in the R.S.A.,
I was born in the R.S.A., born in the R.S.A.

They jailed Mandela, threw away the key
The people struggled to be free
Whites feared they'd be thrown in the sea
We were all freed by the ANC

Madiba's dream has faded now
New fatcats milk the state cash cow
People still in shacks usin' buckets for poo
Cops kill the poor like they used to do

How much better would the D.A. be
They're just a cleaner version of the ANC
This next election's no solution
We need a new grassroots revolution

Kick the B.E.E. pigs from the trough
People! say 'enough's enough!'
Born in the R.S.A., I was born in the R.S.A.,
Born in the R.S.A., rise up again in the R.S.A.

30 January 2014 — The Boss tours here for the first time

6 February 2014 — Putin spends over $50bn on a glitzy Winter Olympics

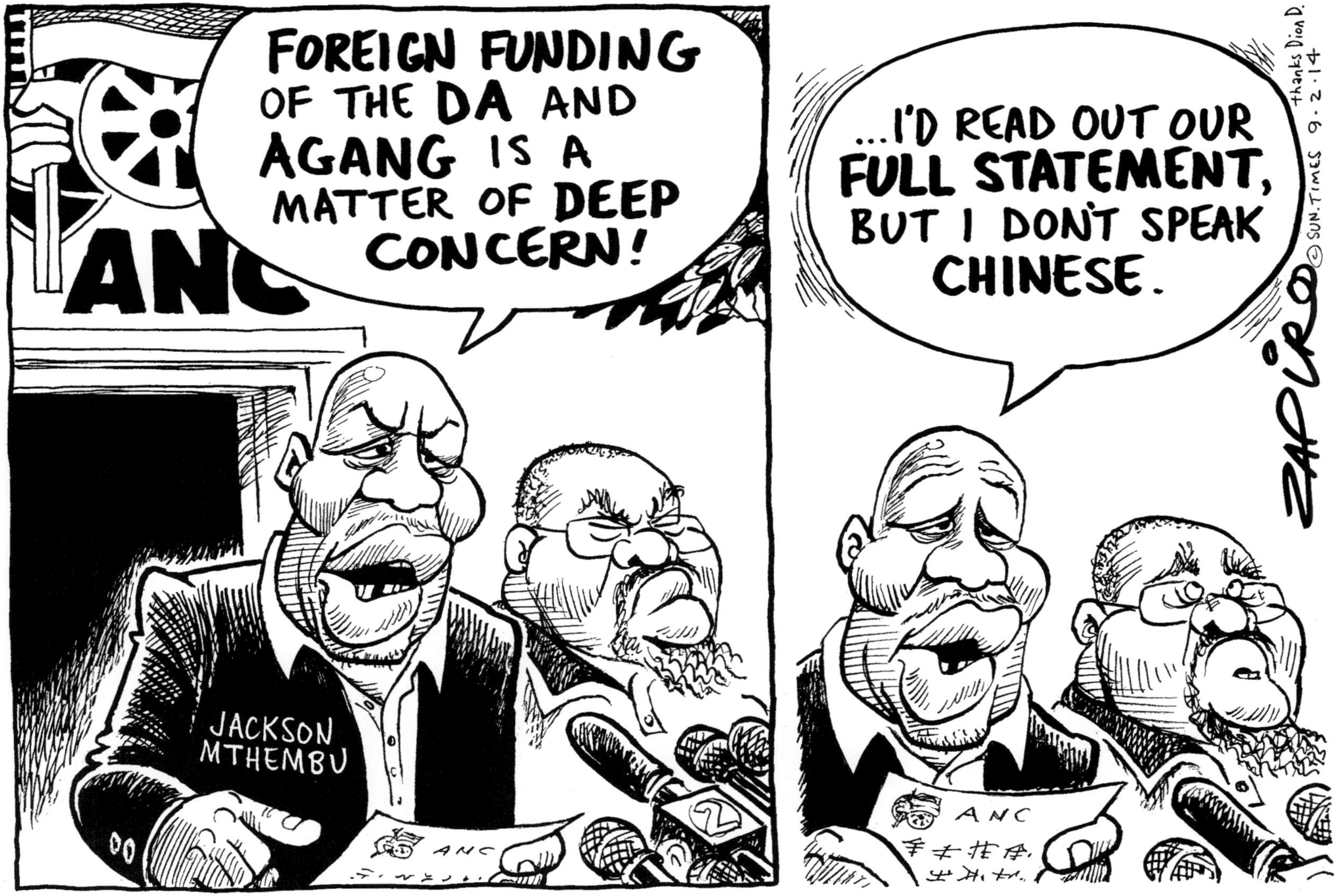
FOREIGN FUNDING OF THE DA AND AGANG IS A MATTER OF DEEP CONCERN!
ANC
JACKSON MTHEMBU
ANC
...I'D READ OUT OUR FULL STATEMENT, BUT I DON'T SPEAK CHINESE.
ANC
thanks Dion D.
© SUN. TIMES 9.2.14
ZAPIRO

9 February 2014 Tut-tutting over opposition parties having undisclosed international donors

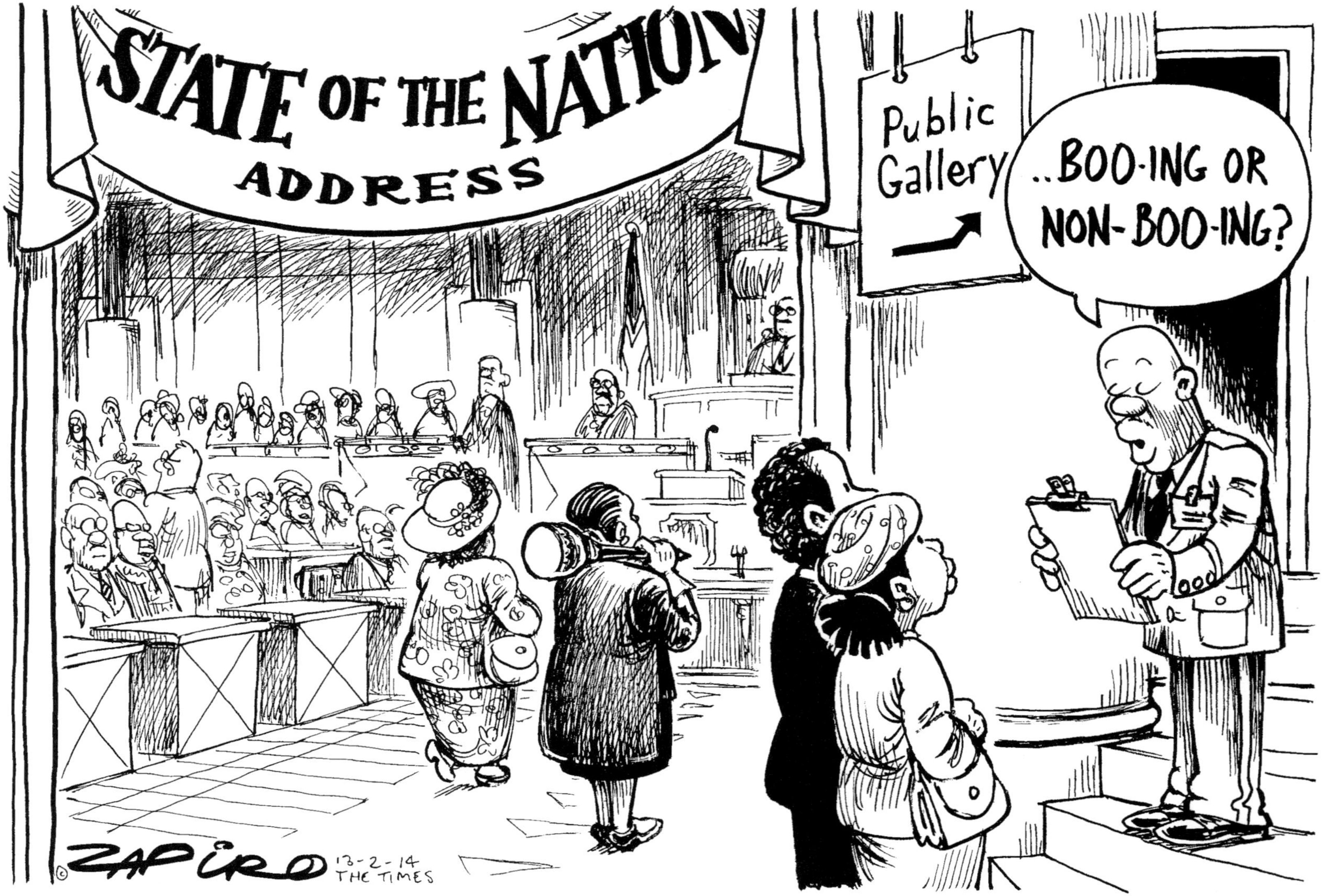
STATE OF THE NATION
ADDRESS
Public Gallery
..BOO-ING OR NON-BOO-ING?
© ZAPIRO 13-2-14 THE TIMES

13 February 2014

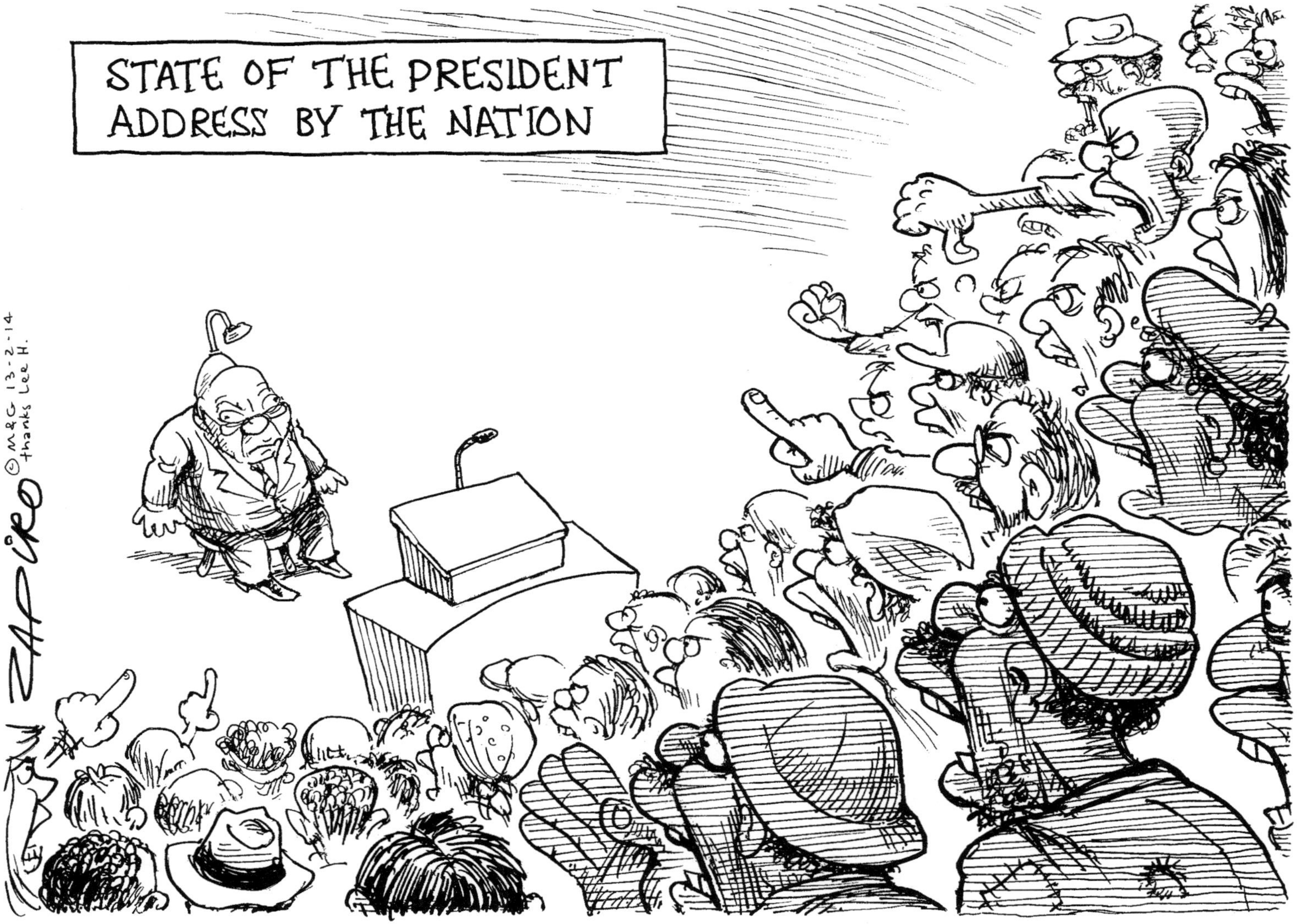
STATE OF THE PRESIDENT ADDRESS BY THE NATION
ZAPIRO
© M&G 13-2-14 thanks Lee H.

13 February 2014

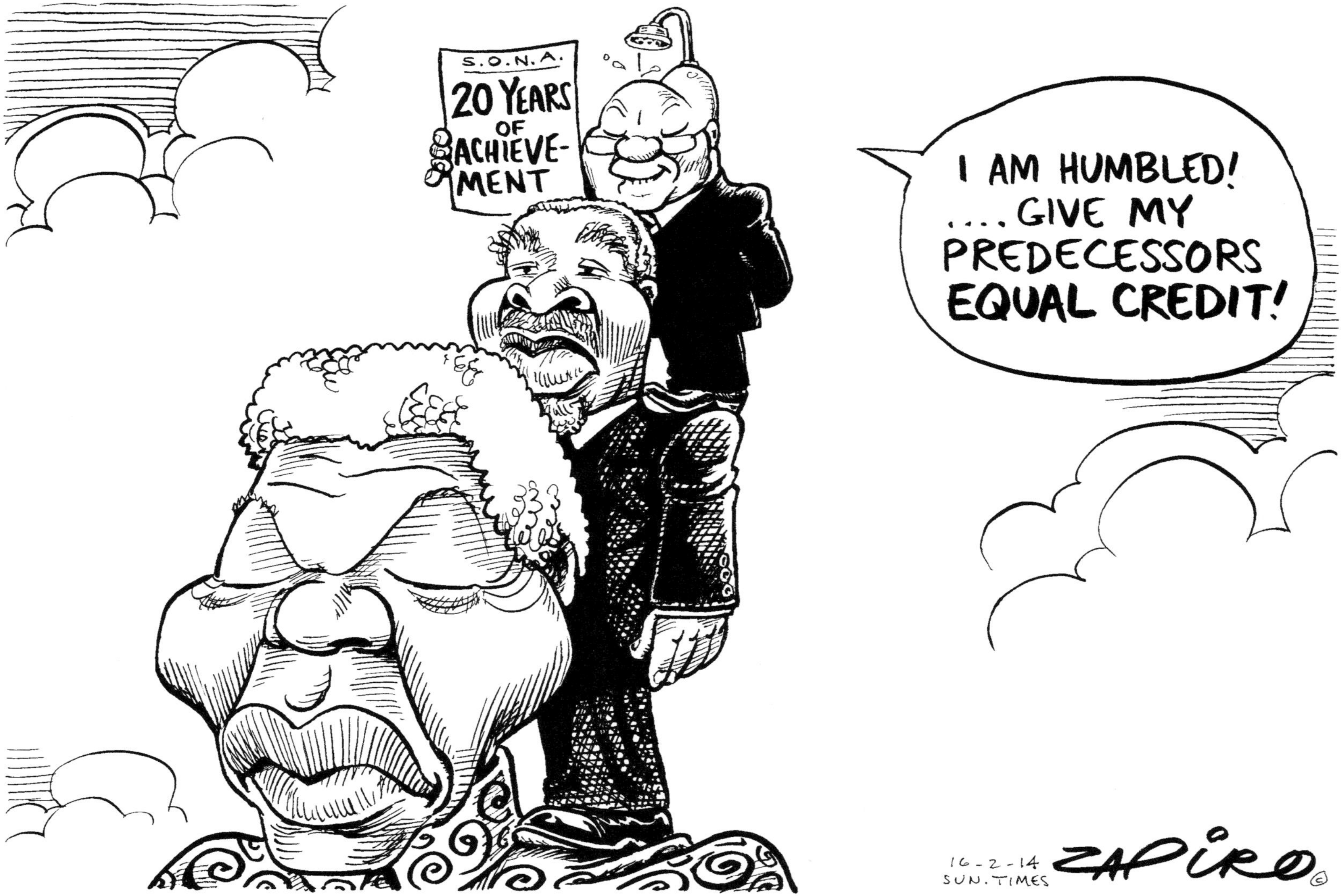
S.O.N.A.
20 YEARS OF ACHIEVEMENT
I AM HUMBLED! ....GIVE MY PREDECESSORS EQUAL CREDIT!
16-2-14
SUN. TIMES
ZAPIRO ©

16 February 2014 His State of the Nation Address punts 'the good story' of the past two decades

Acting head of the public broadcaster is also in her sights

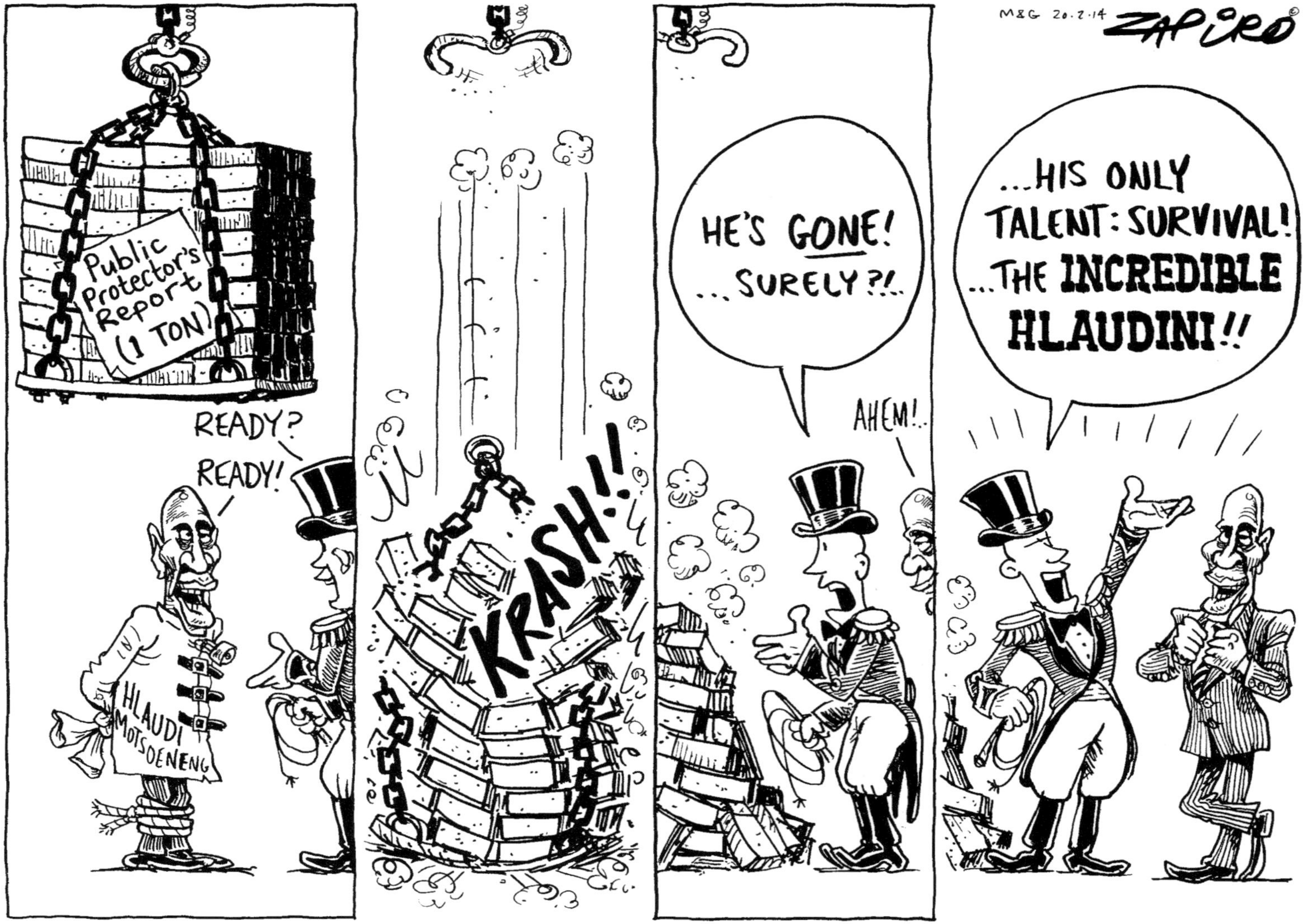
M&G 20.2.14 ZAPIRO©
Public Protector's Report (1 TON)
READY?
READY!
HLAUDI MOTSOENENG
KRASH!!
HE'S GONE! ...SURELY?!
AHEM!..
...HIS ONLY TALENT: SURVIVAL! ...THE INCREDIBLE HLAUDINI!!

20 February 2014

20 February 2014 — Acclaimed primate conservationist Jane Goodall warns Africa about China

23 February 2014 — Zanu-PF spends $1m to celebrate what exactly?

27 February 2014

Uganda's president signs repressive new anti-gay laws. A Kampala tabloid names '200 top homos' even though a similar front-page list in 2011 led to the lynching of a gay activist.

26 February 2014 — Six weeks till voting day

27 February 2014

A court orders that the whole trial can be broadcast live
except for visuals of witnesses who don't agree to be televised

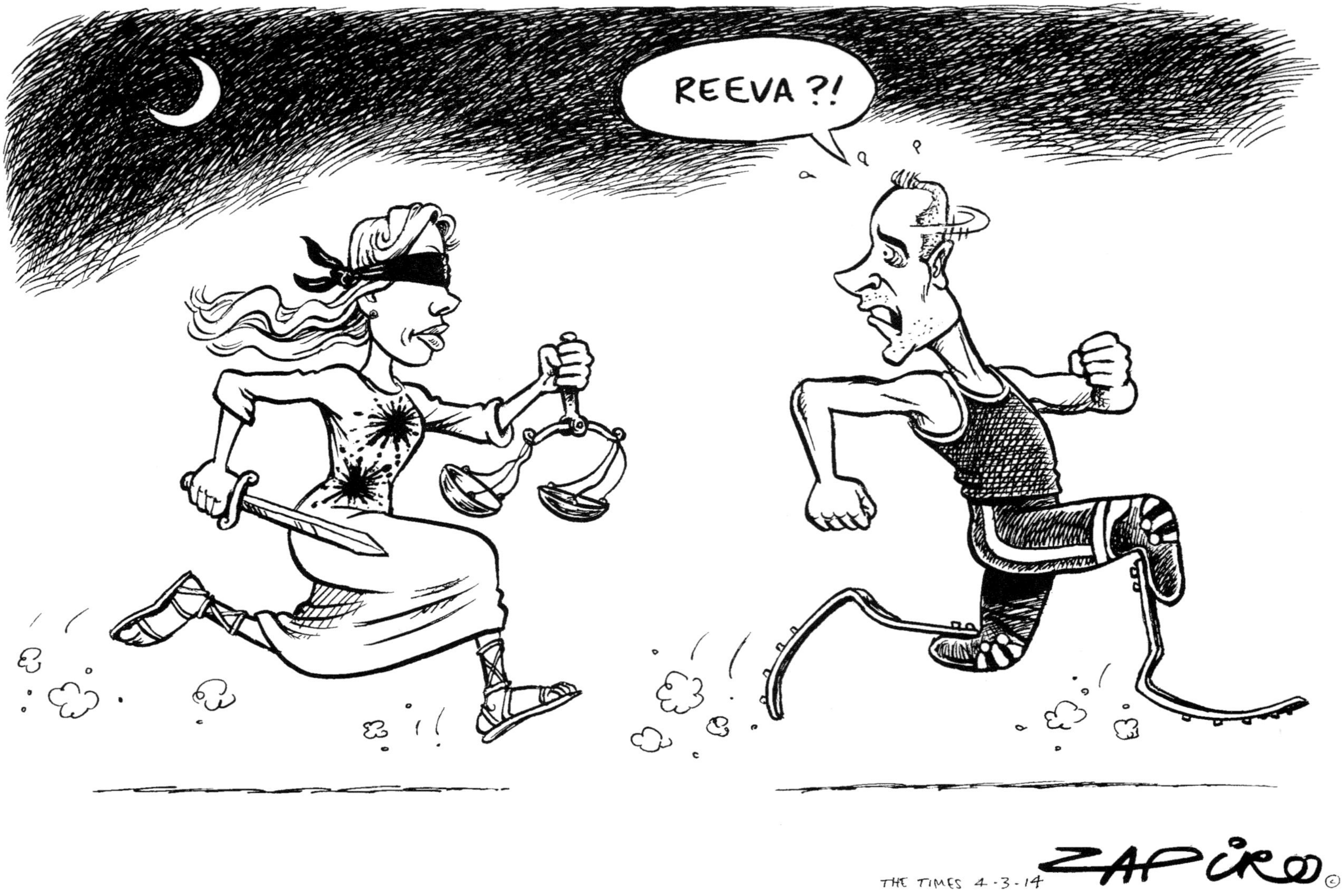
REEVA ?!
THE TIMES 4-3-14
ZAPIRO ©

4 March 2014

Trial begins

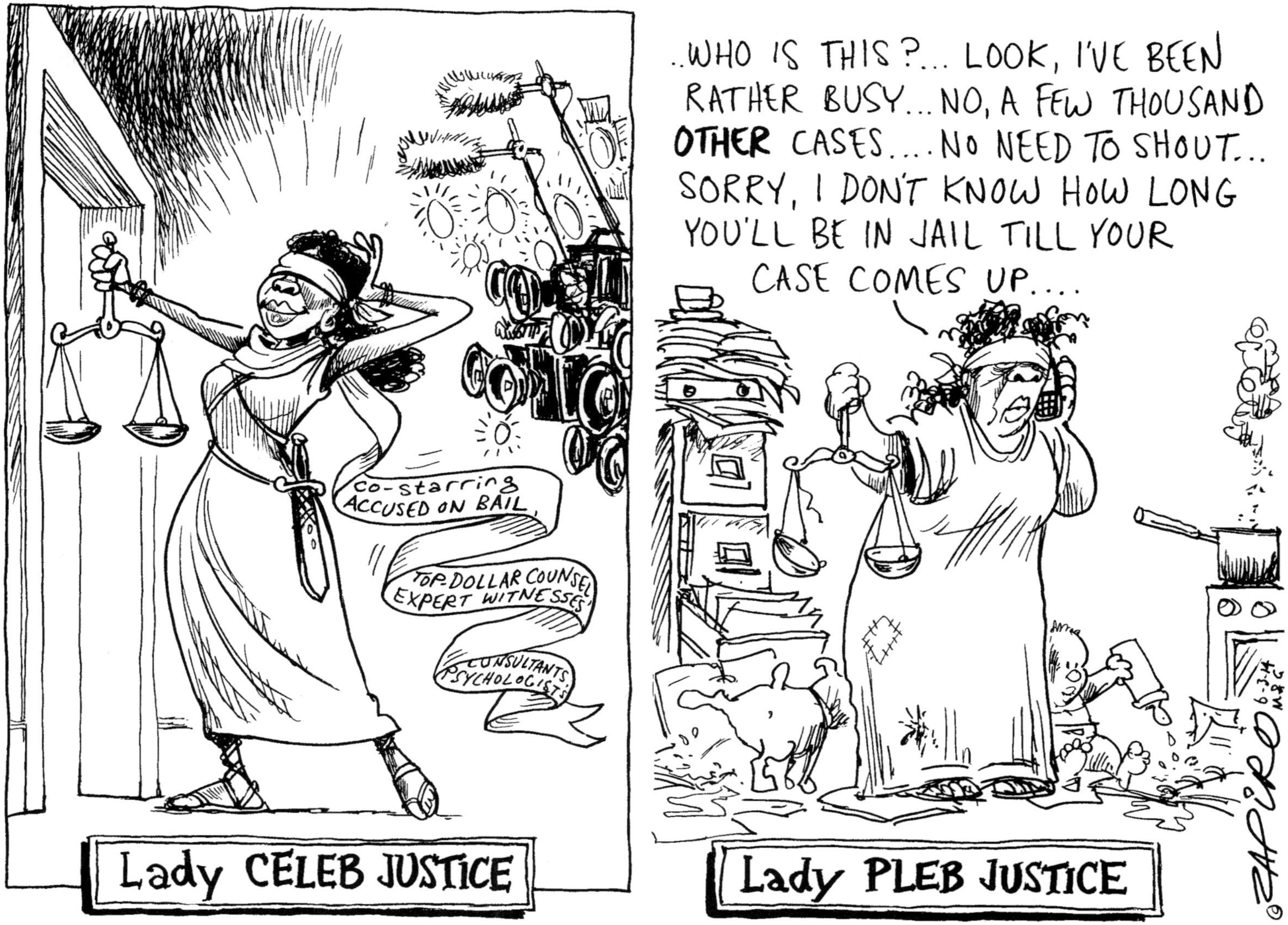
co-starring ACCUSED ON BAIL
TOP-DOLLAR COUNSEL EXPERT WITNESSES
CONSULTANTS PSYCHOLOGISTS
Lady CELEB JUSTICE
..WHO IS THIS?... LOOK, I'VE BEEN RATHER BUSY... NO, A FEW THOUSAND OTHER CASES.... NO NEED TO SHOUT... SORRY, I DON'T KNOW HOW LONG YOU'LL BE IN JAIL TILL YOUR CASE COMES UP....
Lady PLEB JUSTICE
© ZAPIRO

6 March 2014

2 March 2014

Losing it and getting personally abusive on social media with senior *City Press* journalist Carien du Plessis

6 March 2014   The Tsar redux annexes the Crimea, then de-stabilises what remains of his western neighbour

Ahead of the election, struggle stalwarts with real substance, including some on the ANC's Integrity Committee, are leaving parliament or being ignored by the party

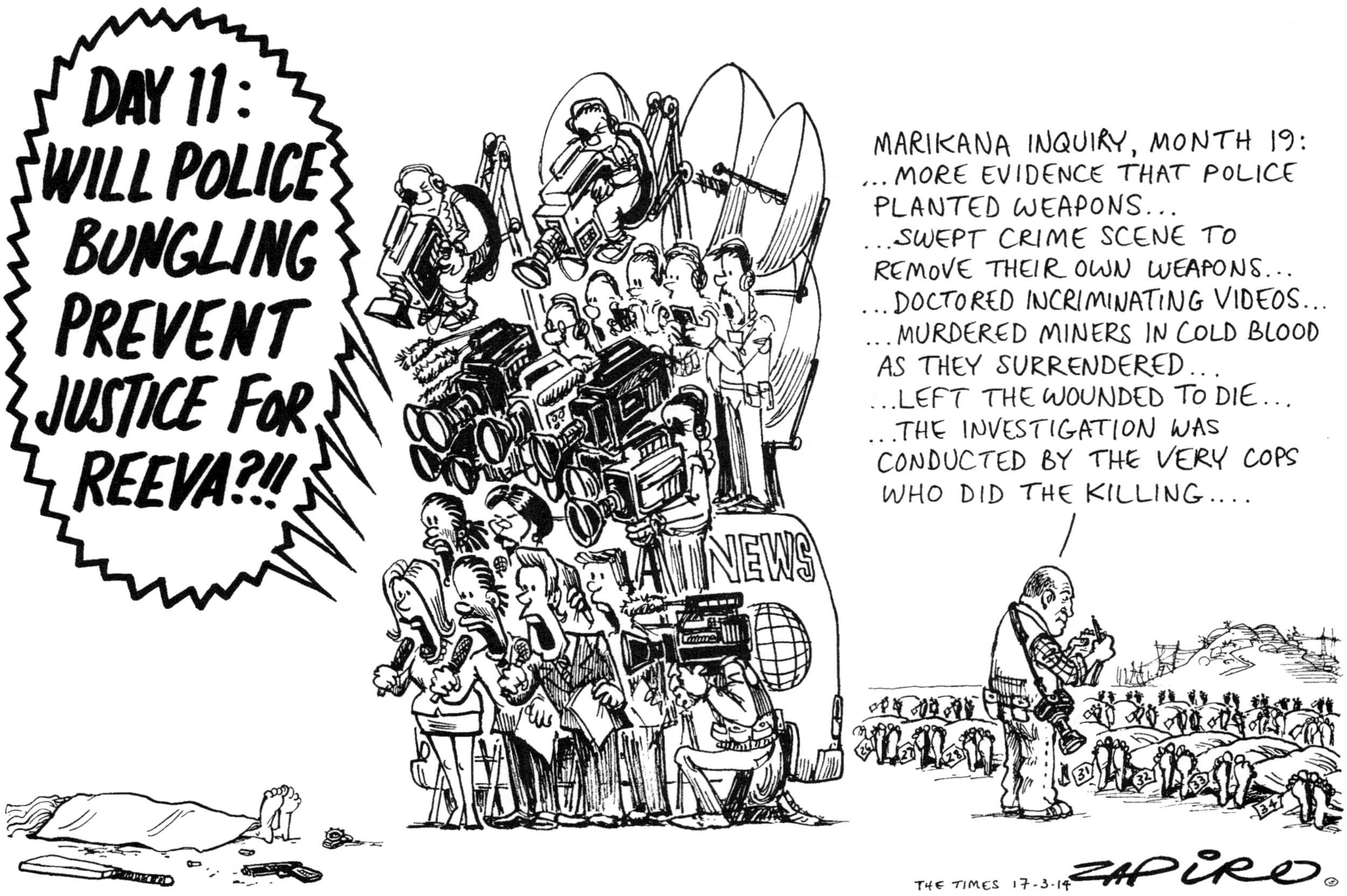
DAY 11: WILL POLICE BUNGLING PREVENT JUSTICE FOR REEVA?!!
NEWS
MARIKANA INQUIRY, MONTH 19: ...MORE EVIDENCE THAT POLICE PLANTED WEAPONS... ...SWEPT CRIME SCENE TO REMOVE THEIR OWN WEAPONS... ...DOCTORED INCRIMINATING VIDEOS... ...MURDERED MINERS IN COLD BLOOD AS THEY SURRENDERED... ...LEFT THE WOUNDED TO DIE... ...THE INVESTIGATION WAS CONDUCTED BY THE VERY COPS WHO DID THE KILLING....
THE TIMES 17-3-14 ZAPIRO ©

17 March 2014

17 March 2014   They tried to block it any way they could but the eagerly awaited document is about to be released

20 March 2014

She finds Zuma and his family improperly benefited from the upgrades,
he violated the Executive Ethics Code and he must pay back some of the money

Predictably, party hacks attack her but so do some independent African church bishops claiming she's part of demonic forces planning to derail the revolution

19 March 2014

23 March 2014 — Her report gives the lie to expensive features like the new chicken run being essential security upgrades

25 March 2014 — Members of the prosecution team have flown to Apple's US headquarters to gain access to encrypted iPhone data – evidence that could be vital

SHRIEN DEWANI'S TOP 10 EXCUSES

10. The cleaning lady threw away my extradition order
9. I had to go to my wife's funeral
8. My alarm clock didn't go off — 1213 times!
7. The laundromat shredded my straitjacket
6. I fell asleep on the psychiatrist's couch
5. The pilot lost his keys
4. I was stuck in air traffic
3. I had an attack of the Shaiks
2. My doctor's flashdrive exploded
1. The dog ate my anti-depressants

28 March 2014 — A different high-profile murder suspect gives up his long London legal battle against extradition

The public protector nailed her for an irregular lease which violates procurement rules yet Pansy still thinks she's the right person to run an election

3 April 2014   Euphemisms abound in the official reports

6 April 2014

High Court rules a DA text message – 'how Zuma stole your money' – is fair comment because of the phrase 'licence to loot' in Madonsela's report

ZOMBIE STOPPER

He says he's never heard of zombie stopper bullets. Then he weeps
as the prosecution shows video of him shooting a watermelon,
laughing about exploding brains and saying 'f*** it's a zombie stopper'.

10 April 2014

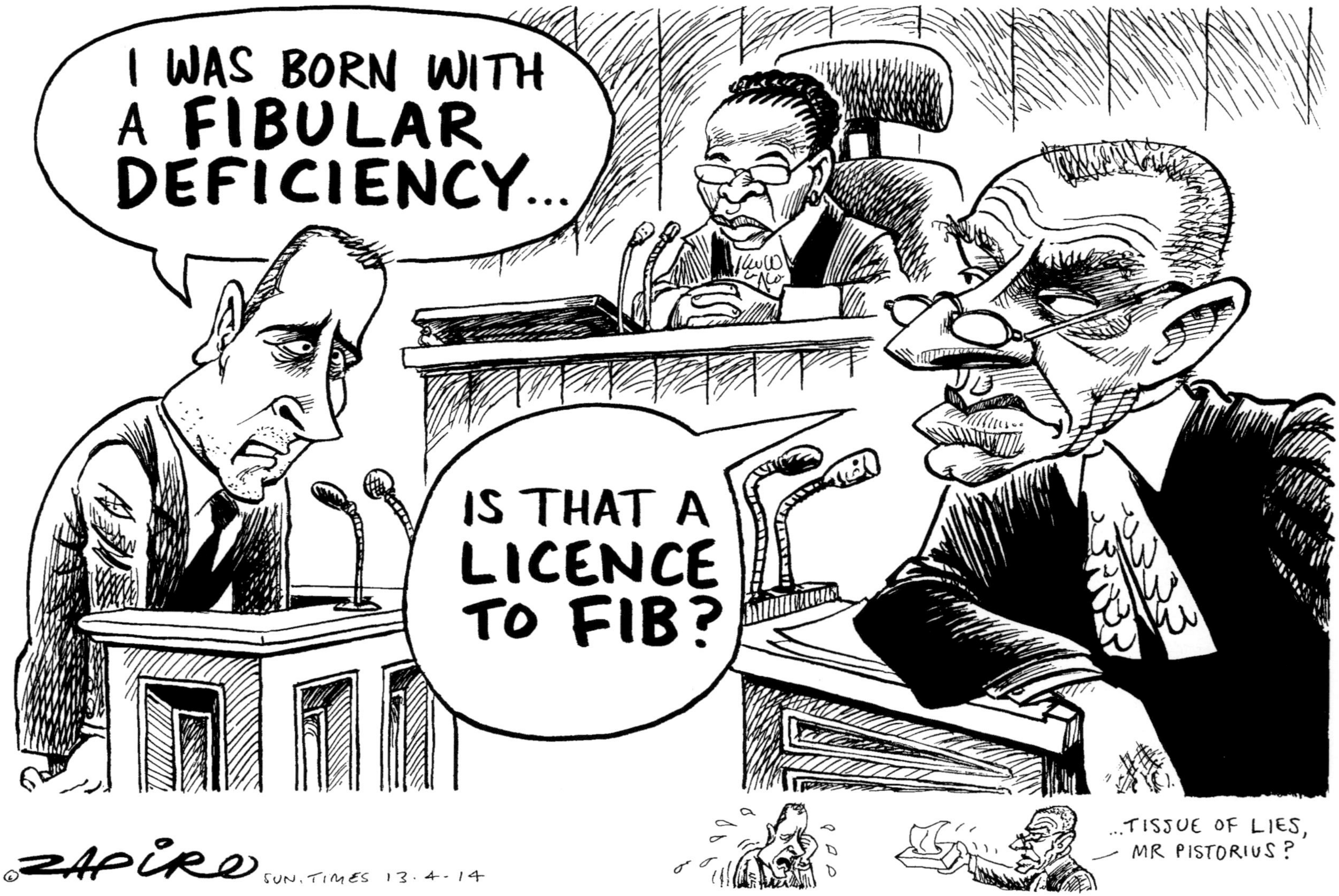
I WAS BORN WITH A FIBULAR DEFICIENCY...
IS THAT A LICENCE TO FIB?
...TISSUE OF LIES, MR PISTORIUS?
©ZAPIRO SUN. TIMES 13-4-14

13 April 2014

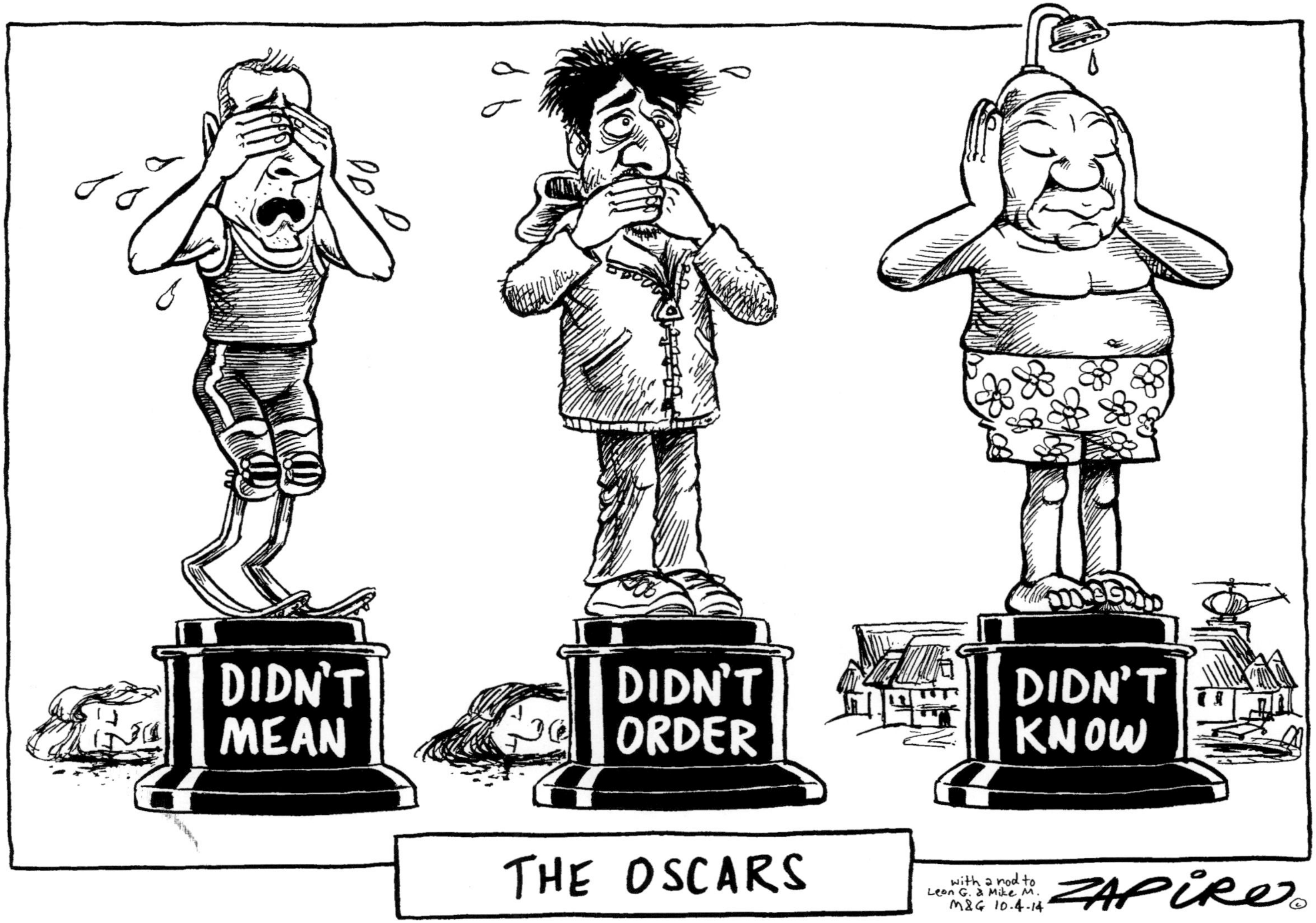
DIDN'T MEAN
DIDN'T ORDER
DIDN'T KNOW
THE OSCARS
with a nod to Leon G. & Mike M. M&G 10-4-14
ZAPIRO ©

10 April 2014

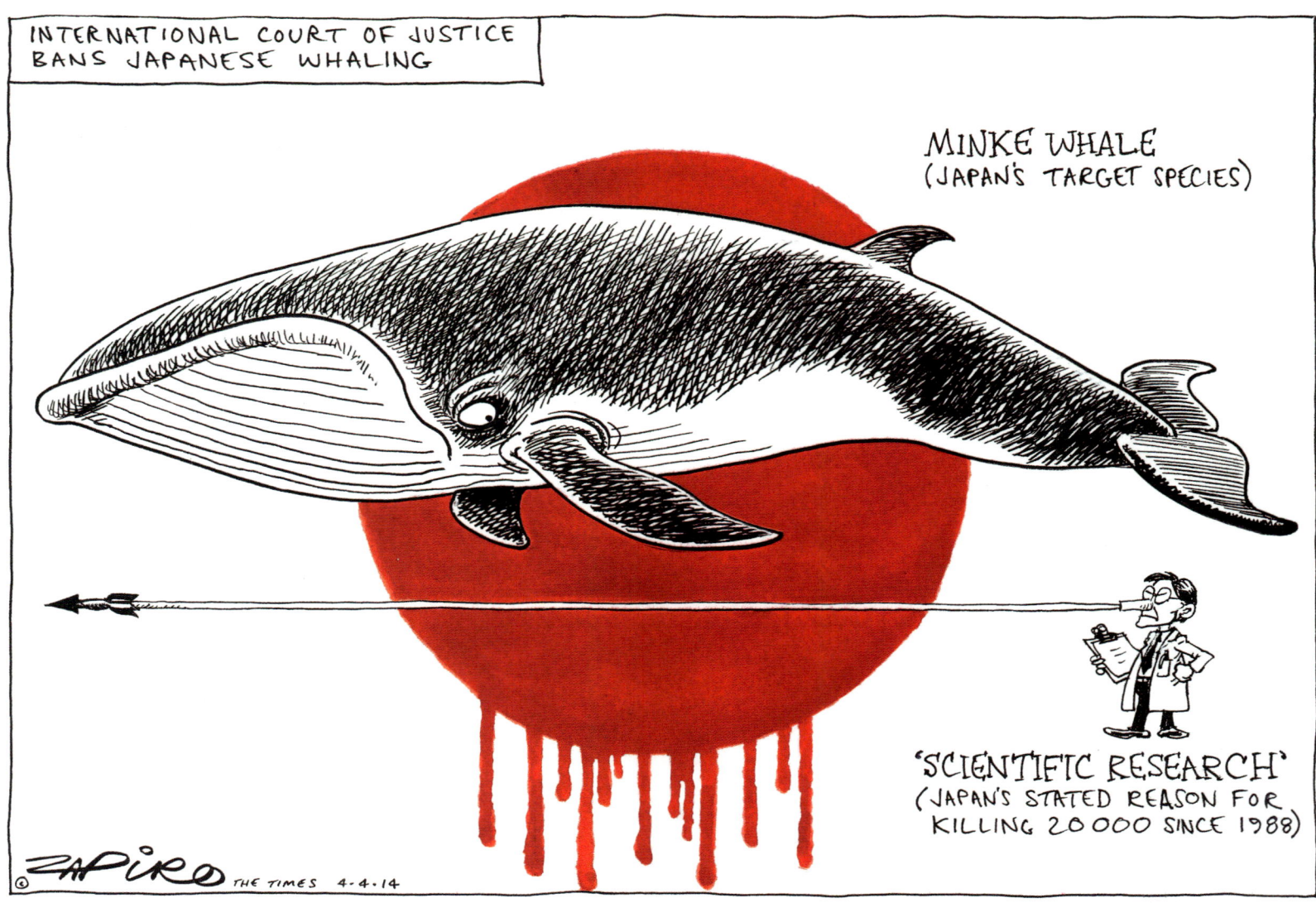

4 April 2014 — Only two credible studies have appeared in nine years of slaughter

8 April 2014 — Multinational bodies hesitate to intervene in the violence between Christians and Muslims in the Central African Republic

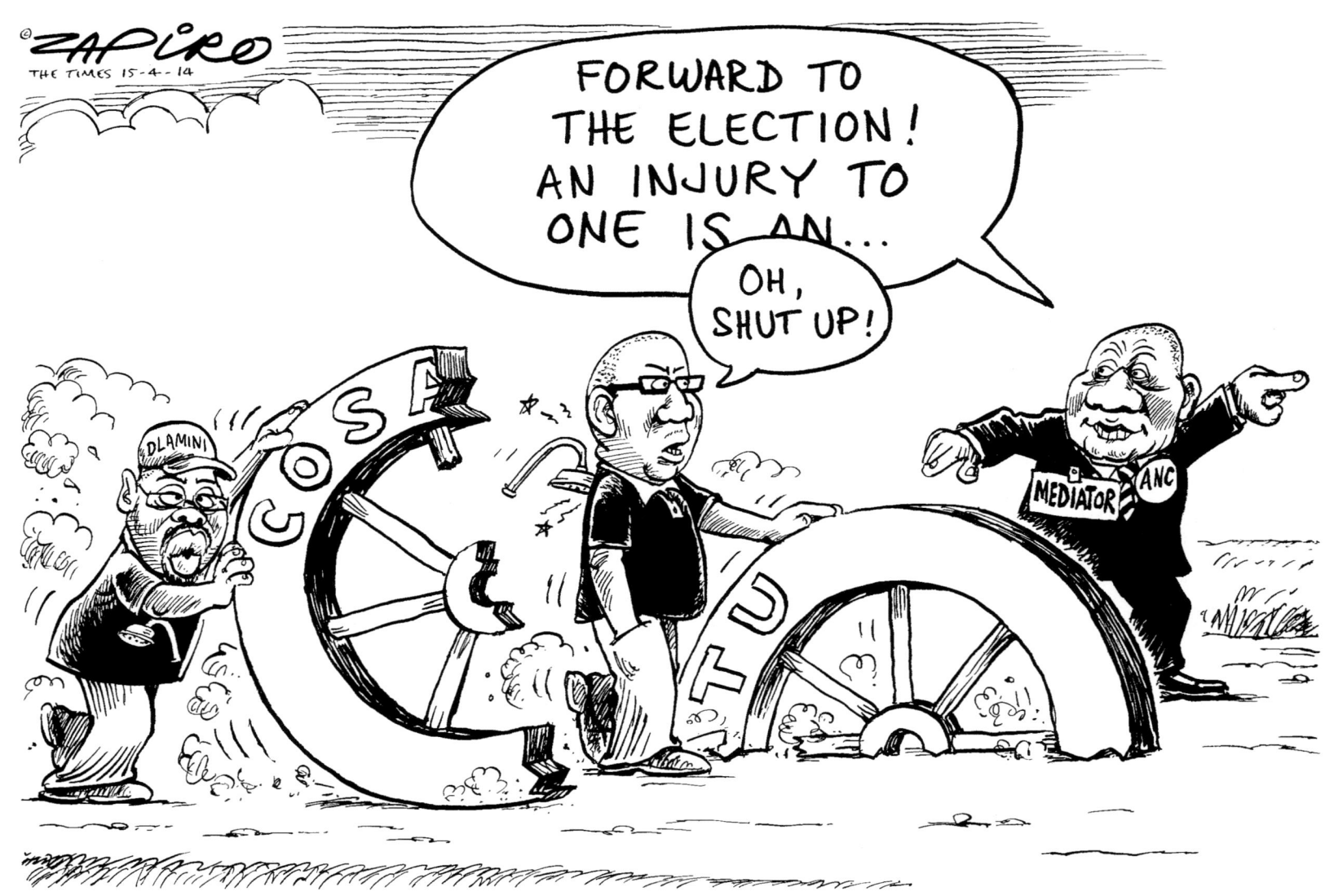

Defying Cosatu president S'dumo Dlamini, suspended general secretary Zwelinzima Vavi wins a court battle for reinstatement. Deputy president Cyril Ramaphosa's been told to smooth things over.

15 April 2014

The Vote No campaign. Ronnie Kasrils calls on ANC supporters to vote for smaller parties or to spoil their ballots.

20 April 2014

Freedom Day. The Arch announces that with a heavy heart he won't be voting ANC this time.

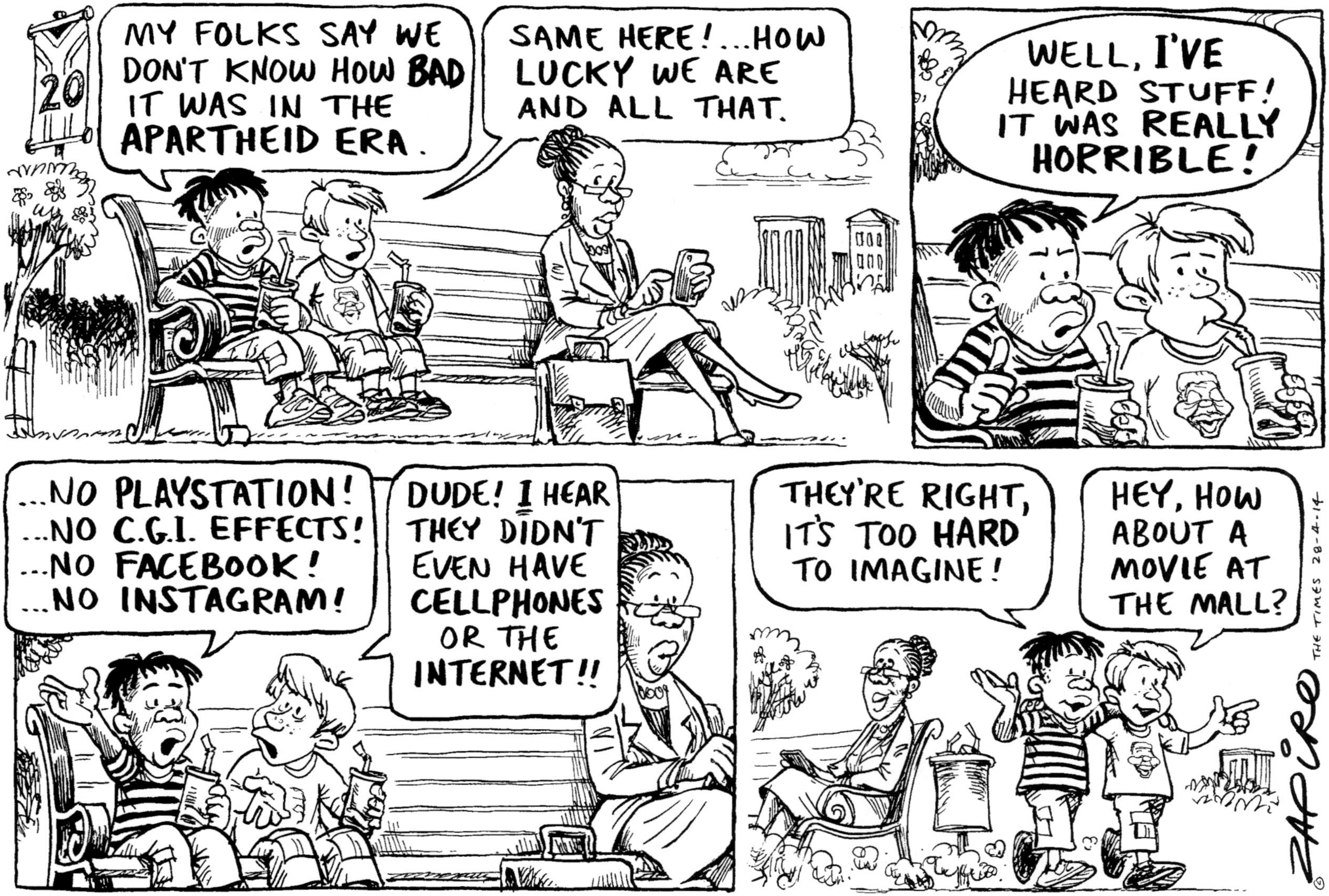
20
MY FOLKS SAY WE DON'T KNOW HOW BAD IT WAS IN THE APARTHEID ERA.
SAME HERE! ...HOW LUCKY WE ARE AND ALL THAT.
WELL, I'VE HEARD STUFF! IT WAS REALLY HORRIBLE!
...NO PLAYSTATION! ...NO C.G.I. EFFECTS! ...NO FACEBOOK! ...NO INSTAGRAM!
DUDE! I HEAR THEY DIDN'T EVEN HAVE CELLPHONES OR THE INTERNET!!
THEY'RE RIGHT, IT'S TOO HARD TO IMAGINE!
HEY, HOW ABOUT A MOVIE AT THE MALL?
THE TIMES 28-4-14
ZAPIRO ©

28 April 2014

Fifth democratic election

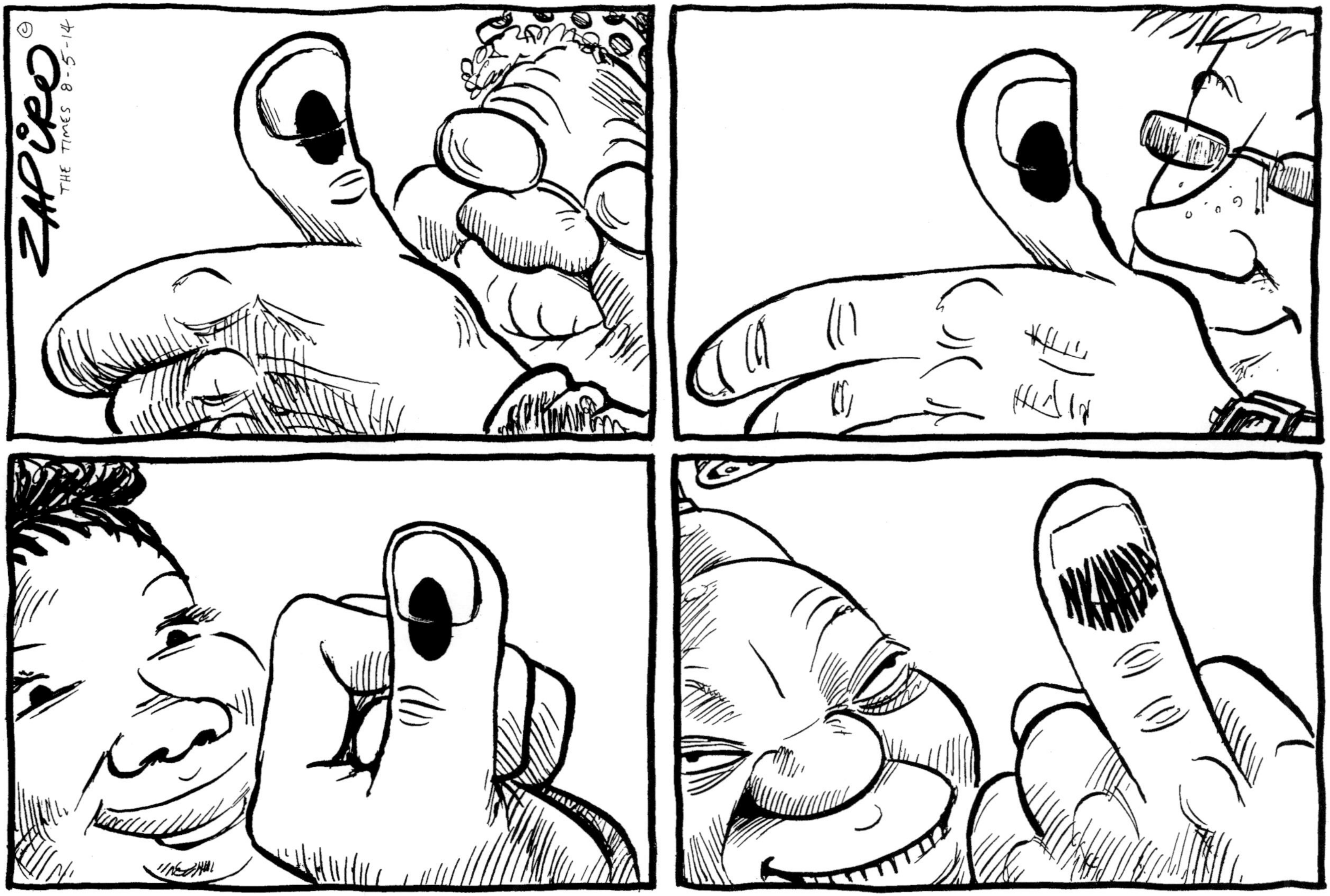
ZAPIRO ©
THE TIMES 8-5-14
NKANDLA

8 May 2014

Results are in – ANC gets 60%

8 May 2014

But they dropped 3%, support is fading fast in major metropoles and two opposition parties are on the rise

11 May 2014 — The populist wins 6%, his new party is now the third biggest

The DA's Mazibuko leaves parliament to study in the USA

Huffy about the sudden departure, she attacks Mazibuko's track record and character — a former DA official says the party is ruled by fear

21 May 2014

22 May 2014 — Dress code flouted, worker outfits flaunted, EFF stress the parliamentary system from day one

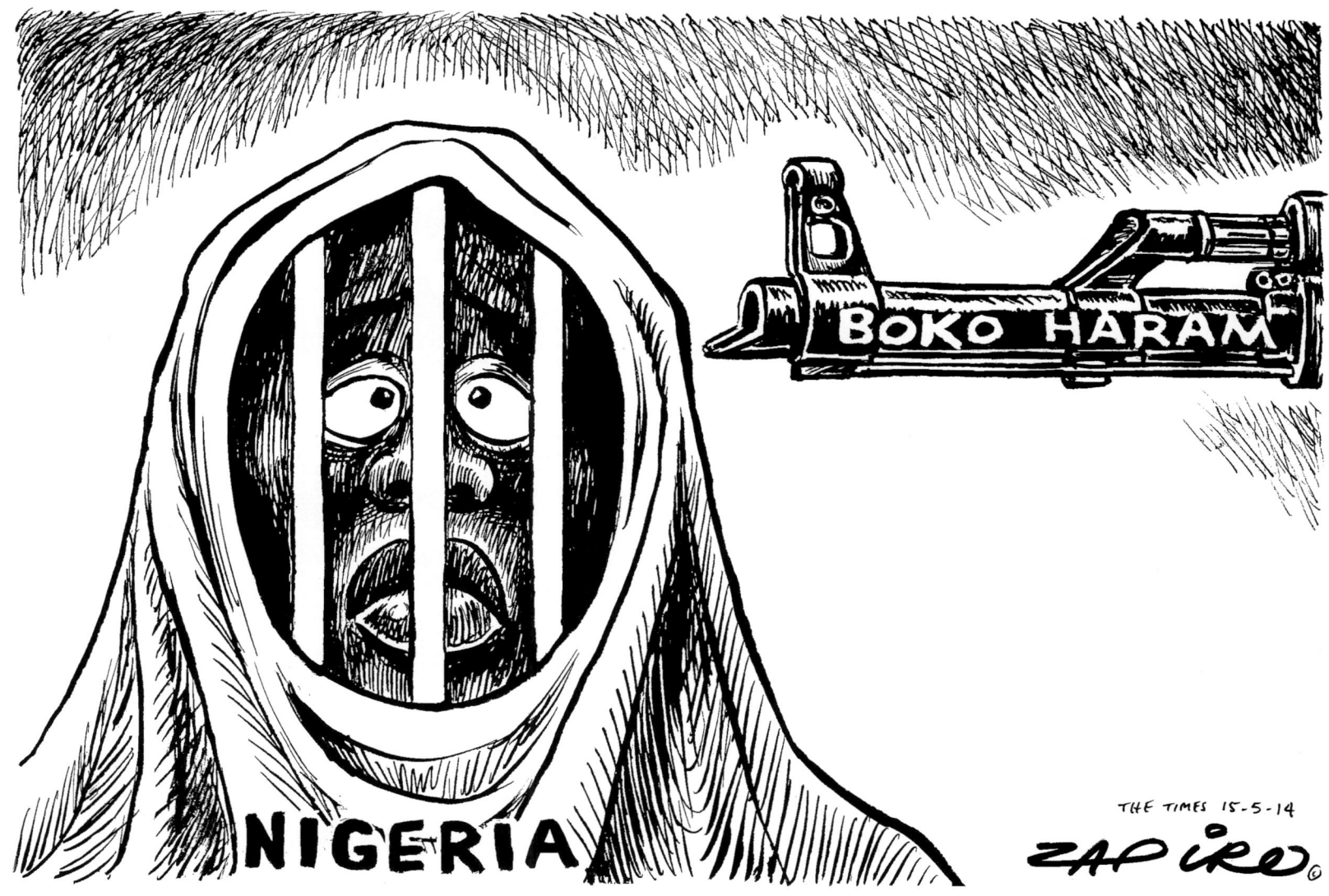

276 Nigerian schoolgirls kidnapped by Islamic extremists, inept local authorities seem powerless to rescue them, #BringBackOurGirls gains traction on Twitter

22 May 2014

Party deputy secretary-general Jessie Duarte says it's unacceptable that only one of eight ANC-appointed provincial leaders is female

25 May 2014 — Swearing-in of second-term president. And reality TV's biggest 'star' marries Kanye West.

27 May 2014 — Pravin Gordhan's replacement is famous for his chair malfunction during an SABC TV interview

29 May 2014 A weird job shift for Nathi Mthethwa whose term as police minister is infamous for police brutality

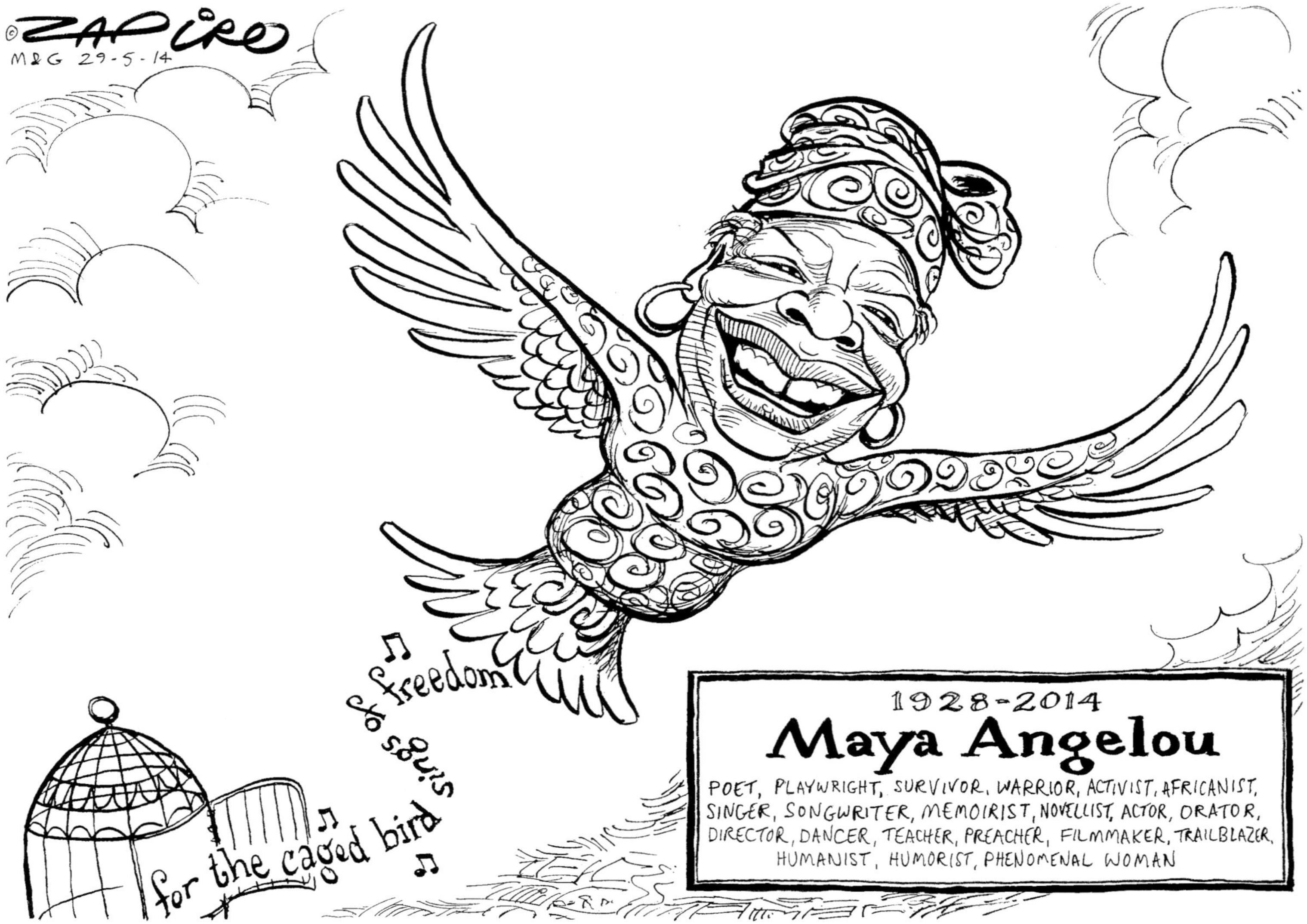
©ZAPIRO
M&G 29-5-14
♫ freedom
of sings
for the caged bird ♫
1928-2014
Maya Angelou
POET, PLAYWRIGHT, SURVIVOR, WARRIOR, ACTIVIST, AFRICANIST, SINGER, SONGWRITER, MEMOIRIST, NOVELLIST, ACTOR, ORATOR, DIRECTOR, DANCER, TEACHER, PREACHER, FILMMAKER, TRAILBLAZER, HUMANIST, HUMORIST, PHENOMENAL WOMAN

29 May 2014

1 June 2014 — Scary comments from Mogoeng Mogoeng about laws that run against the essence of his religious beliefs

5 June 2014 — His explanations just make things worse

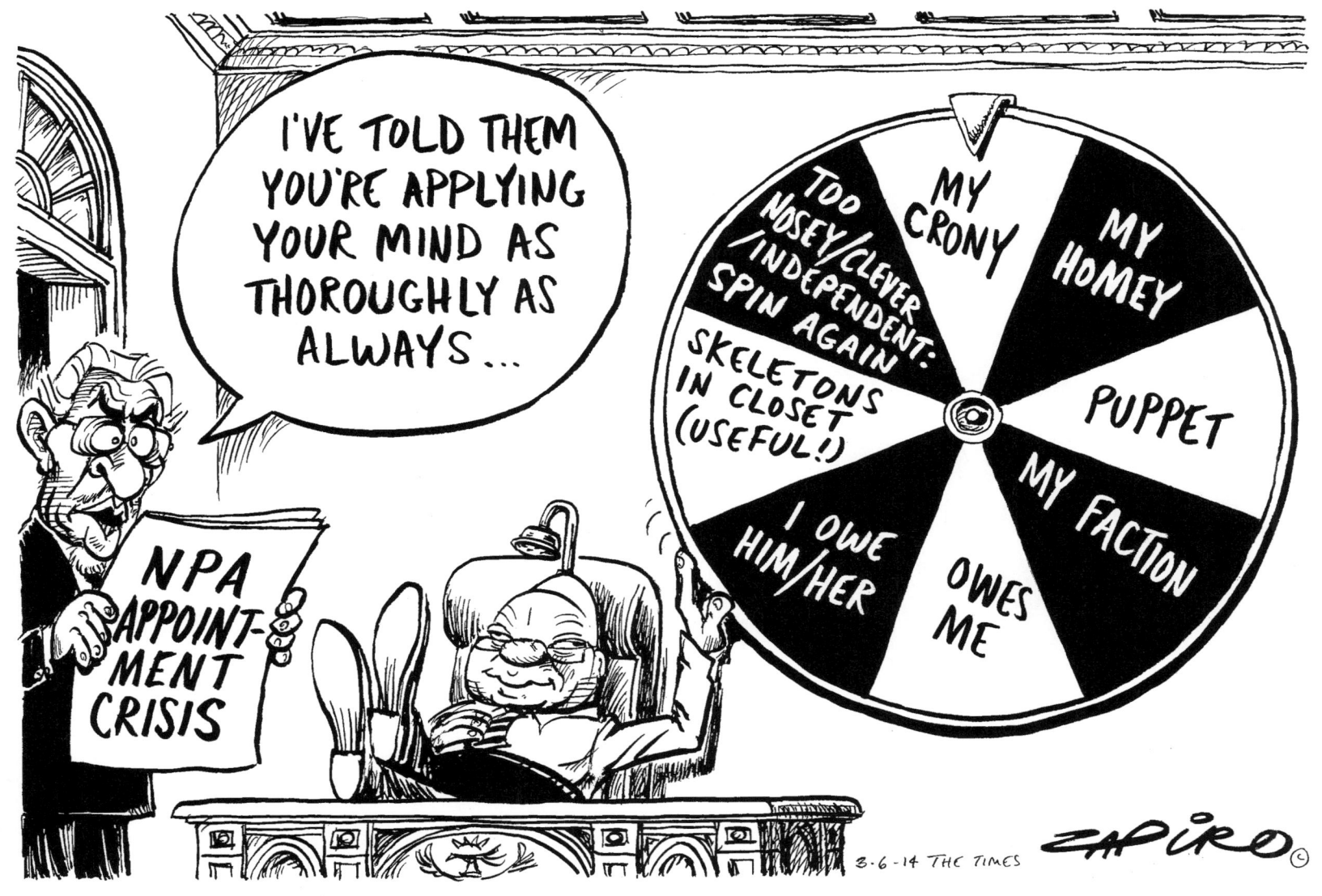

Another blunder. Zuma's latest choice to run the National Prosecuting Authority, Mxolisi Nxasana, is denied security clearance because he failed to declare an old murder charge.

8 June 2014

5 June 2014

Hash replaces Graeme Smith to become our first black Proteas' captain as Victor leaps out of retirement to be interim Bok leader while Jean de Villiers recovers from injury

Violent street protests spread as Brazil spends three times what we did in 2010 to host Sepp Blatter's World Cup

8 June 2014

Will he see out his second term? Health rumours and disgruntlement within the party fuel the theory that Cyril will replace him.

19 June 2014

Malema sets the tone for the new parliament by mocking the president's commitments to clean up corruption and provide millions of jobs

22 June 2014 — Champion of the poor who leads a luxury lifestyle

During a visit to Venda, traditional leaders give the SABC boss
a cow and a calf ... and a bevy of women from whom he selects a bride

26 June 2014

Bust twice before for biting, the Uruguayan striker this time sinks his teeth into the shoulder of Italy's Giorgio Chiellini during a World Cup group game

Soccer bosses move fast on the biting. Less so on
bribery allegations around the 2022 World Cup hosting rights for Qatar.

29 June 2014

Under court-ordered observation for a month at Weskoppies to determine whether he has general anxiety disorder

Three editors and other senior staffers resign from *Independent*.
When the *Cape Times* editor he sacked is given the prestigious
Nat Nakasa award by her peers, Survé storms out of the ceremony.

3 July 2014

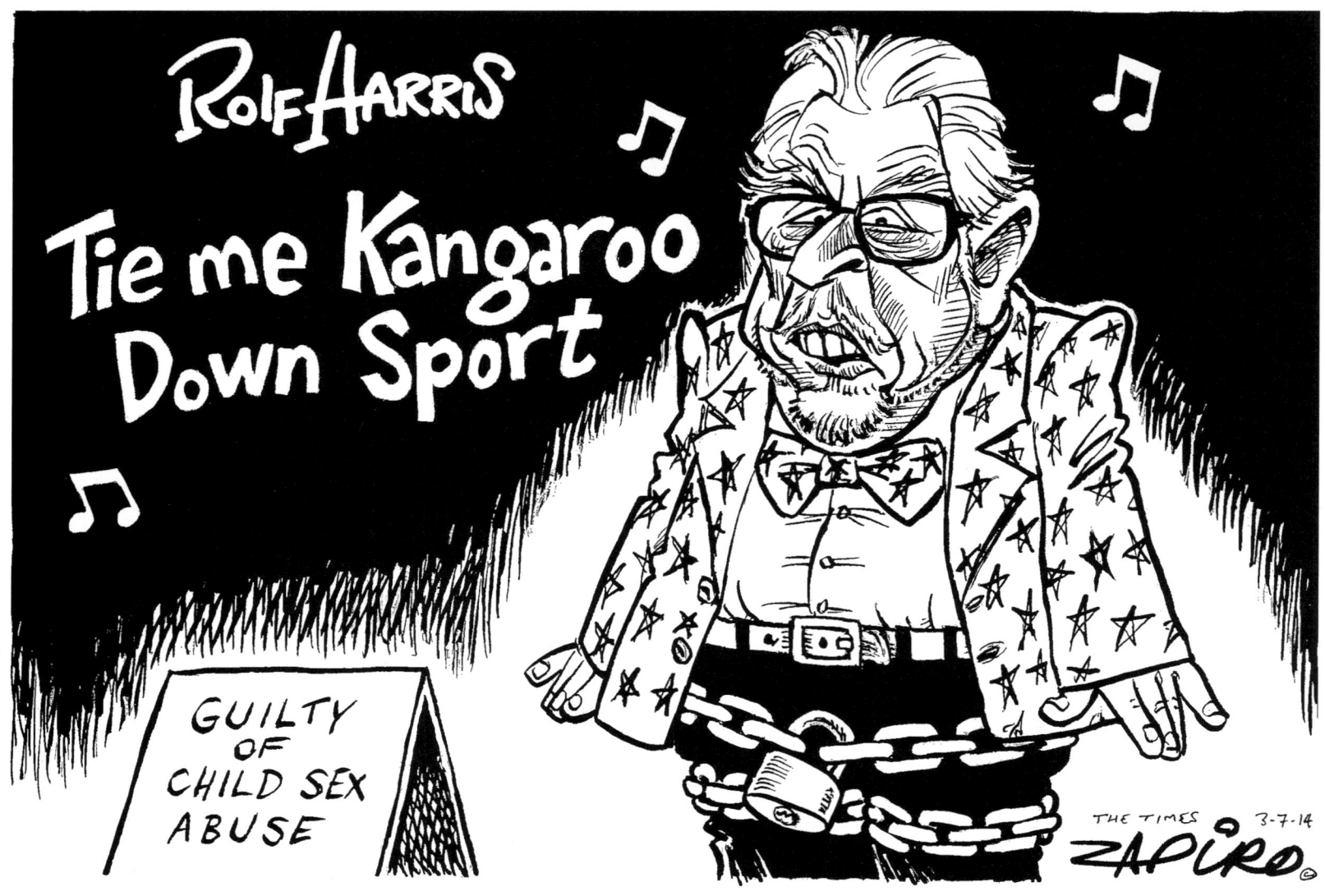

3 July 2014 — UK jury finds the legendary Aussie entertainer guilty of 12 charges of indecently assaulting young girls

6 July 2014

Another Motsoeneng moment – the acting SABC boss proposes that journalists be officially regulated like doctors and lawyers

10 July 2014

Who cares about his string of controversies, mismanagement, self-enrichment and Madonsela's damning report? New communications minister Faith Muthambi makes him permanent COO.

10 July 2014 — A record 7−1 annihilation of the World Cup hosts by Germany

13 July 2014   Match-up in the Maracanã – can Argentina's boyish wonder overcome the titanic Teutons?

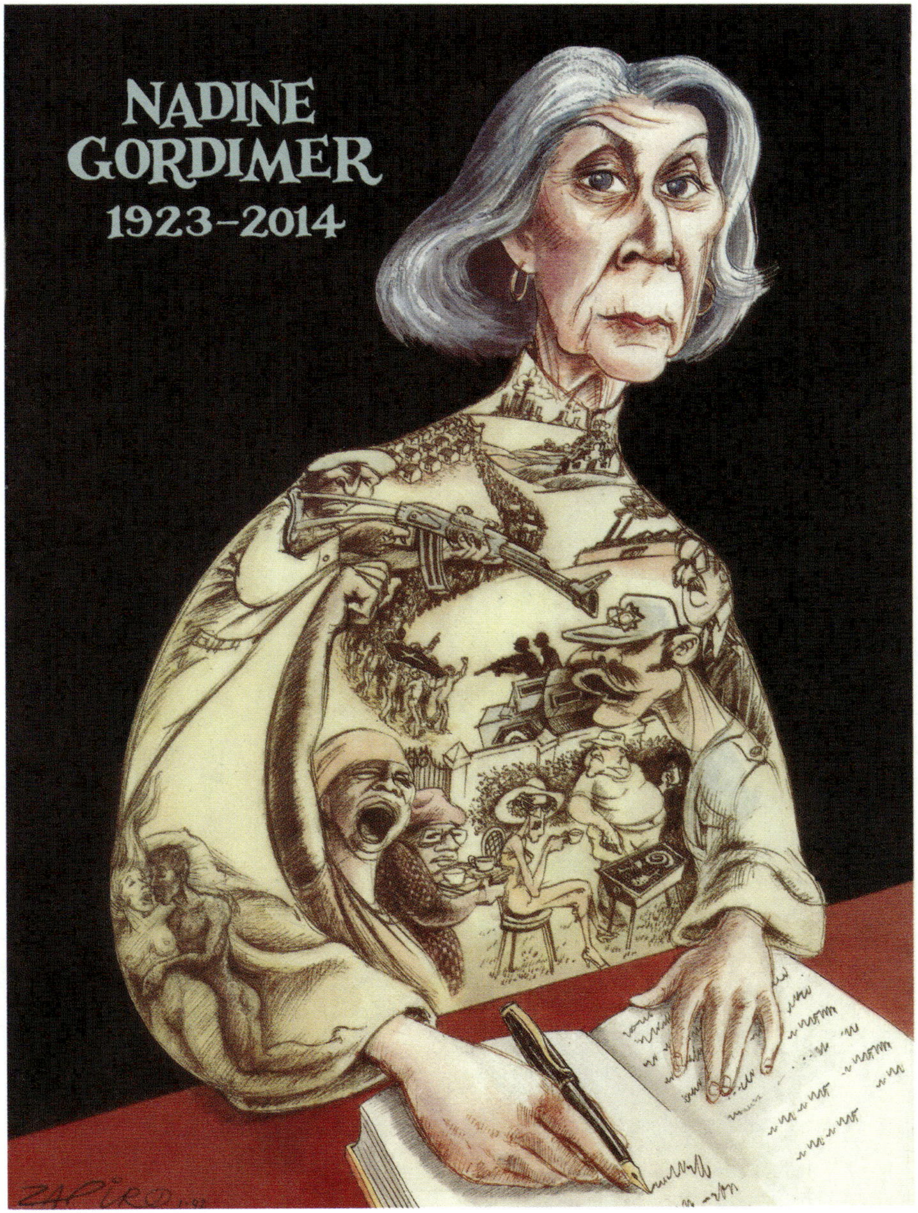
NADINE
GORDIMER
1923–2014

15 July 2014, The Times

Thandi Modise, NCOP chairperson and ANC bigwig, plays the blame game when reports reveal that over 200 animals had either starved to death or been put down by the SPCA on her neglected farm where workers were paid shameful wages

17 July 2014

17 July 2014 — After nine days of conflict, the death toll from Israeli strikes on Gaza passes 200, including four young boys who were shelled while on a beach

Malaysian airliner crashes in the Ukraine killing 298. Everything points towards a Russian missile fired by Russian-backed separatists. Putin is unfazed by the evidence and the global outrage.

22 July 2014

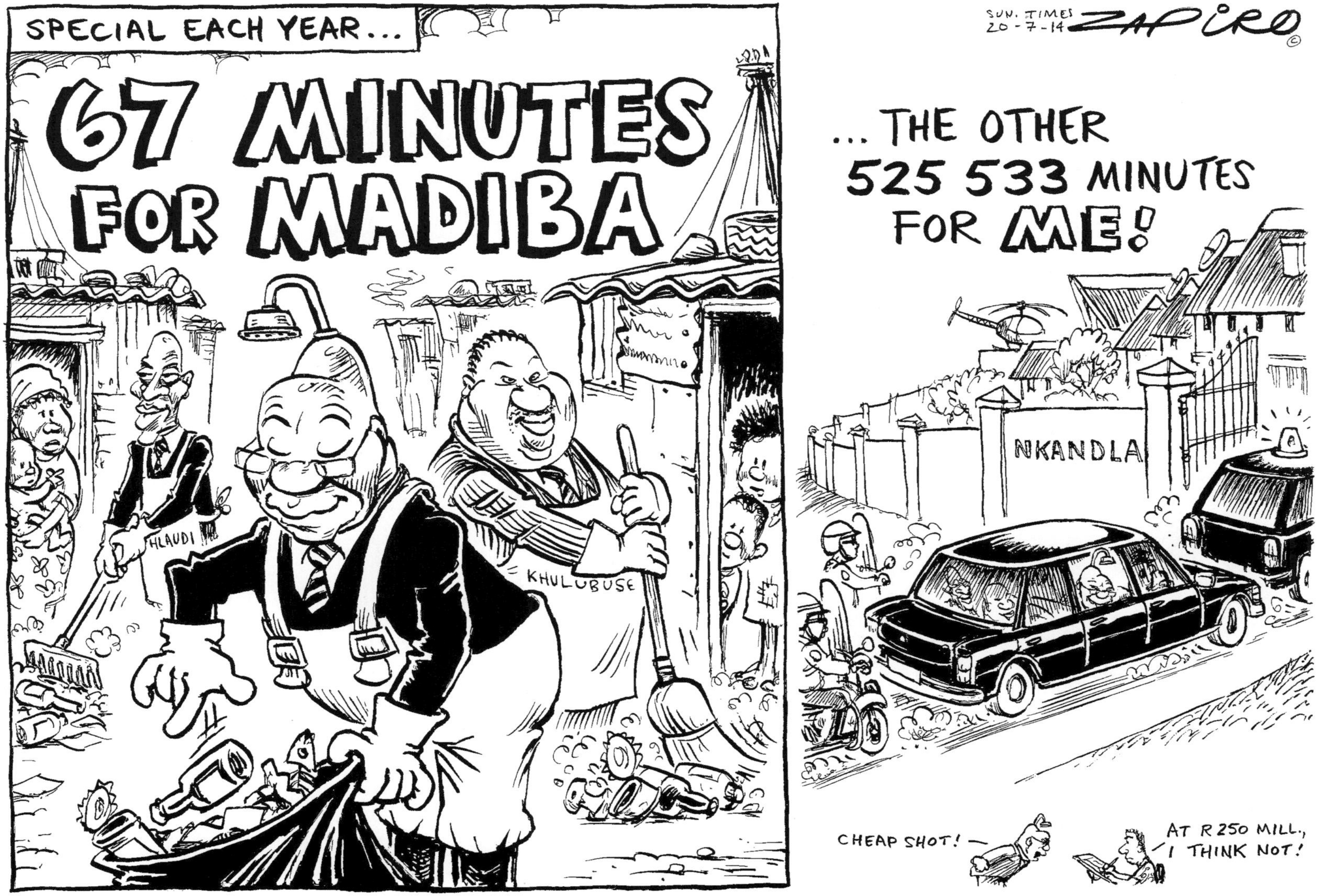
SPECIAL EACH YEAR...
67 MINUTES FOR MADIBA
HLAUDI
KHULUBUSE
SUN. TIMES 20-7-14 ZAPIRO ©
...THE OTHER 525 533 MINUTES FOR ME!
NKANDLA
CHEAP SHOT!
AT R250 MILL., I THINK NOT!

20 July 2014

Mandela Day

24 July 2014

Expelled for wearing their signature kit, EFF storm the Gauteng legislature and are met by cops in riot gear firing rubber bullets and stun grenades

Shouting match as land reform minister Gugile Nkwinti tables his budget. Labelled a land thief by his long-time foe Andile Mngxitama, Pieter Groenewald counters that blacks stole the land from the Khoi and the San.

24 July 2014

27 July 2014 After only one month in parliament the demagogic populists are calling the tune

In Glasgow, the half-cocked sports minister says Durban will bid big money to host the games in eight years' time — except he hasn't got agreement from his own government

29 July 2014

31 July 2014 — Israel says it's giving civilians in Gaza advance warning of impending strikes

At the age of just 25, the president's daughter Thuthukile becomes the youngest-ever head of a minister's office

Open warfare within the prosecuting authority in the form of law suits, media leaks, politicking and allegations of affairs

3 August 2014

The toll road administrator resists Cape Town City's legal bid to force them to reveal financial details of their plans for the province

6 August 2014

An intruder! Finger trouble! Nerves! … he keeps changing his defence under prosecution grilling over why he fired four shots and not just one.

7 August 2014

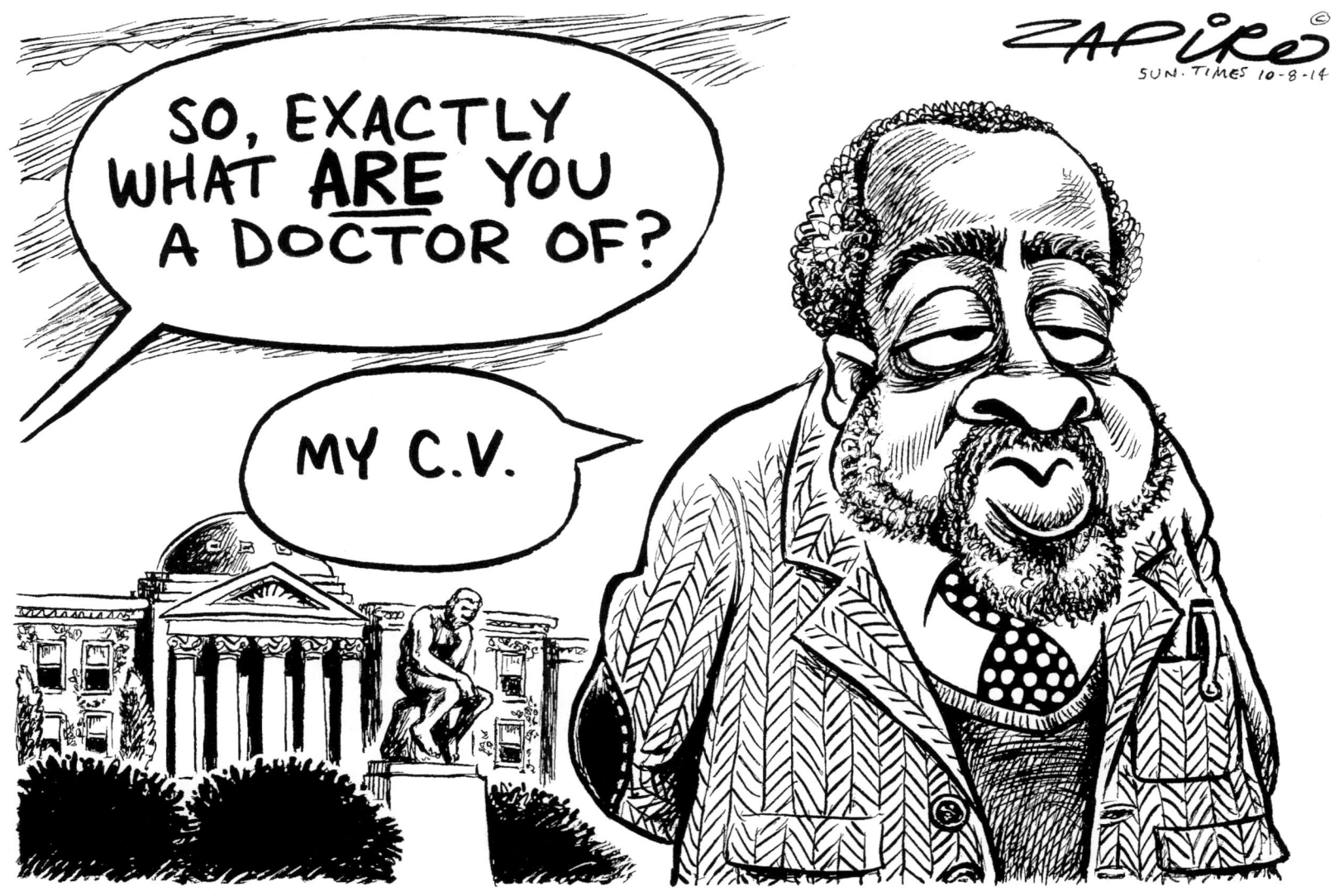

A week after the first report in the *Sunday Times* that he had falsely claimed his academic title, Pallo Jordan remains silent

10 August 2014

Two advocates are the latest to quit judge Willie Seriti's commission of inquiry as it discards key evidence

12 August 2014

At the Farlam Commission into the Marikana Massacre: derided by miners as Buffalo Head over his lavish game auction bids, the unionist turned billionaire mine boss and deputy president concedes little

14 August 2014

Special Investigating Unit goes after Nkandla architect
Minenhle Makhanya for the over-spending but ignores everyone else

14 August 2014

After fighting for years, the president's lawyers concede in court that they have no legal grounds for blocking the DA's access to the tapes which were key to getting corruption charges against him withdrawn

19 August 2014

21 August 2014 — Contracts unilaterally terminated for striking actors on SABC's most popular and lucrative show

21 August 2014 — Asian tourism to the entire continent plummets after the regional Ebola outbreak

Pay back the money, shout Malema & co. in parliament.
Speaker Baleka Mbete suspends the sitting and calls security to evict the EFF.

26 August 2014

The hashtag takes off on social media just as Julius appears in court to answer some tough financial questions of his own

When Thuli sends Zuma a note criticising his response to her Nkandla report and demanding that he pay back some of the money, she's accused of overstepping her powers and dictating to the legislature

28 August 2014

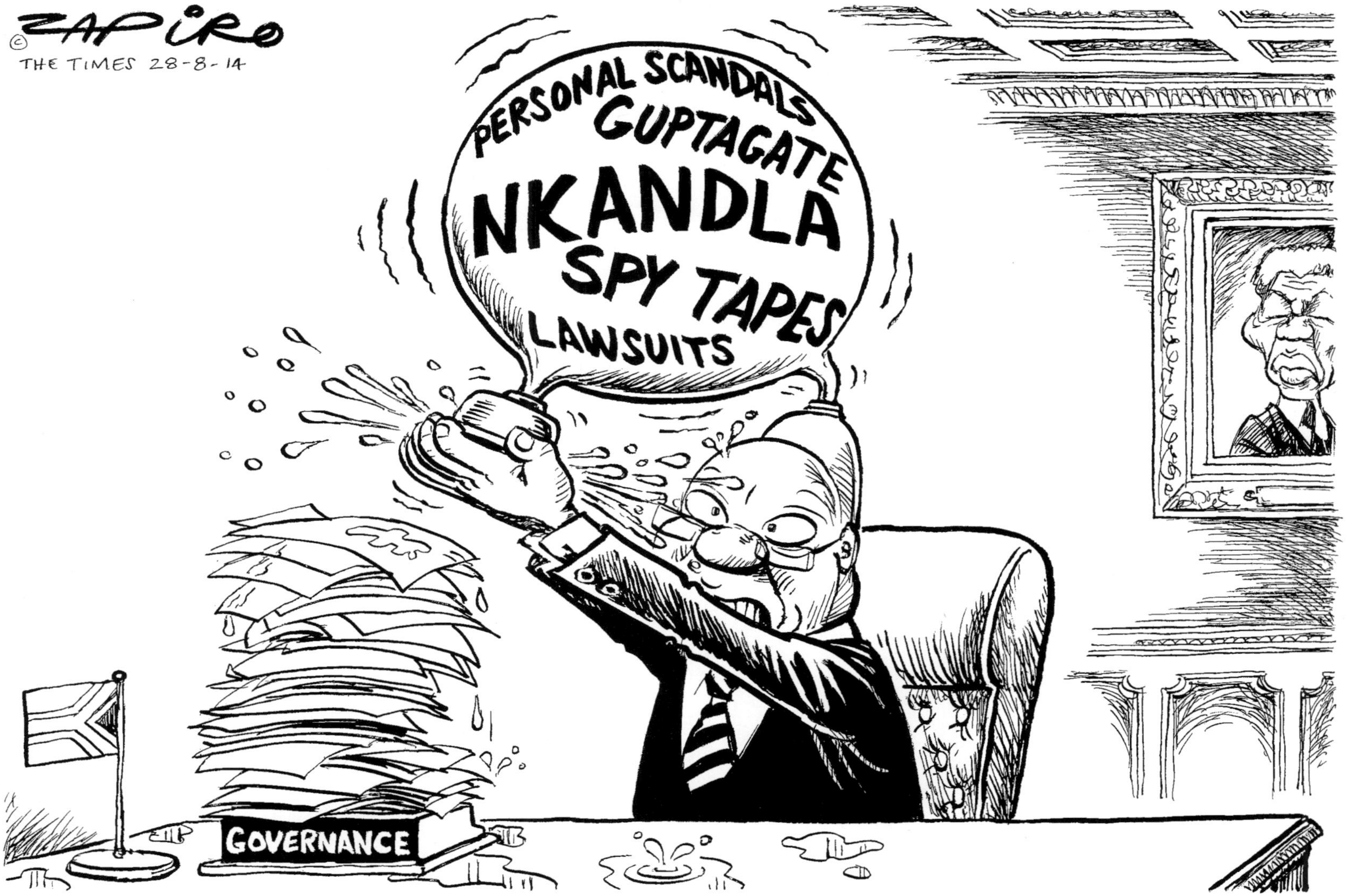
ZAPIRO
© THE TIMES 28-8-14
PERSONAL SCANDALS
GUPTAGATE
NKANDLA
SPY TAPES
LAWSUITS
GOVERNANCE

28 August 2014

31 August 2014   Madonsela was one of Zuma's first major appointments way back in 2009

Protected from coup plotters by South African security forces, Lesotho's prime minister comes to Pretoria for an emergency summit

4 September 2014 — The paranoid president purges three more top spies

The public protector, the Electoral Court and now the Constitutional Court have all ruled against IEC boss Pansy Tlakula. Finally she steps down.

5 September 2014

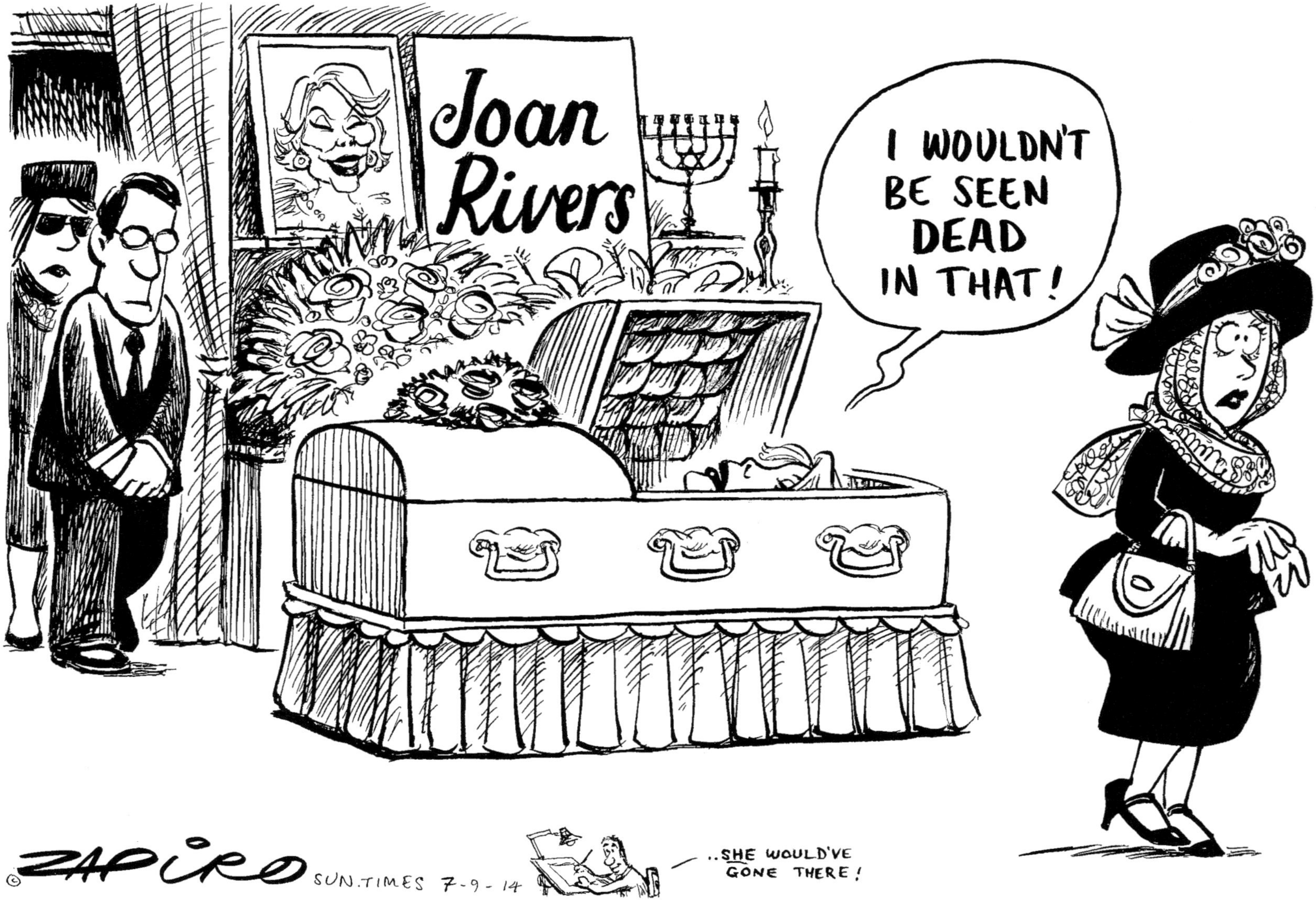
Joan Rivers
I WOULDN'T BE SEEN DEAD IN THAT!
ZAPIRO SUN.TIMES 7-9-14
..SHE WOULD'VE GONE THERE!

7 September 2014

9 September 2014

Wanting to attend a summit of Nobel Peace Laureates in Cape Town, the Dalai Lama is once again denied a visa

British Prime Minister is in a panic after opinion polls show he might lose the Scottish independence referendum

Astonishment from legal experts and the public when Judge Thokozile Mapisa finds Pistorius didn't have the required *dolus eventualis* or understanding of the likely consequences of firing his shots – he's not guilty of murder, just culpable homicide

14 September 2014

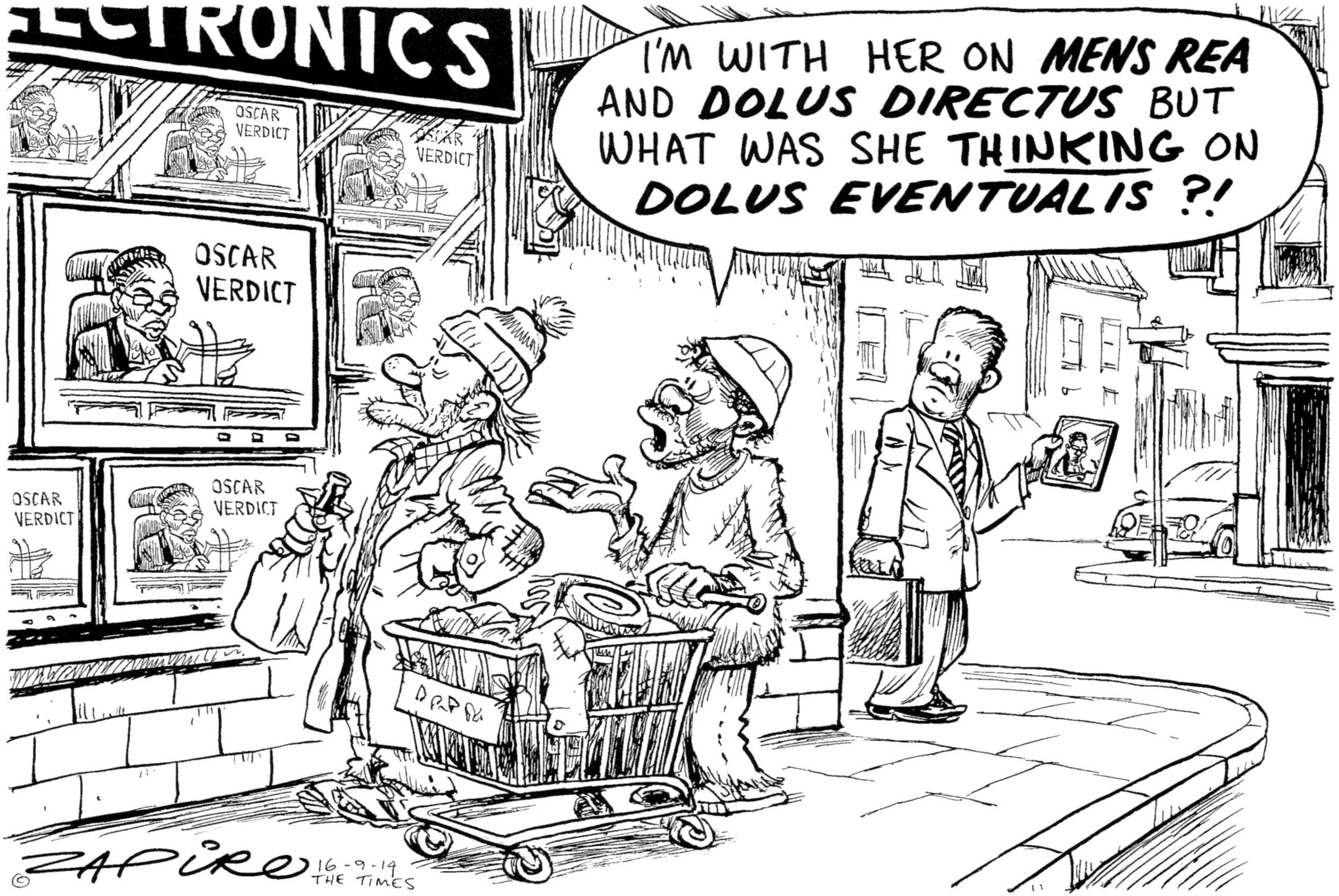

ECTRONICS
OSCAR VERDICT
OSCAR VERDICT
OSCAR VERDICT
OSCAR VERDICT
OSCAR VERDICT
I'M WITH HER ON MENS REA AND DOLUS DIRECTUS BUT WHAT WAS SHE THINKING ON DOLUS EVENTUALIS ?!
© ZAPIRO 16-9-14 THE TIMES

16 September 2014

Gargantua's Wedding

18 September 2014

Thousands attend the extravagant Nkandla nuptials of the president's nephew
(and disgraced empowerment mine owner) to a Swazi princess who is one of his four fiancées

19 September 2014

Over 80 South Africans and many others die in the collapse of a poorly built Lagos megachurch run by the televangelist faith healer, who promptly blames a mysterious low-flying aircraft

Joshua's Synagogue Church of All Nations has a Jo'burg branch
and he's coming to pray for the victims of the disaster

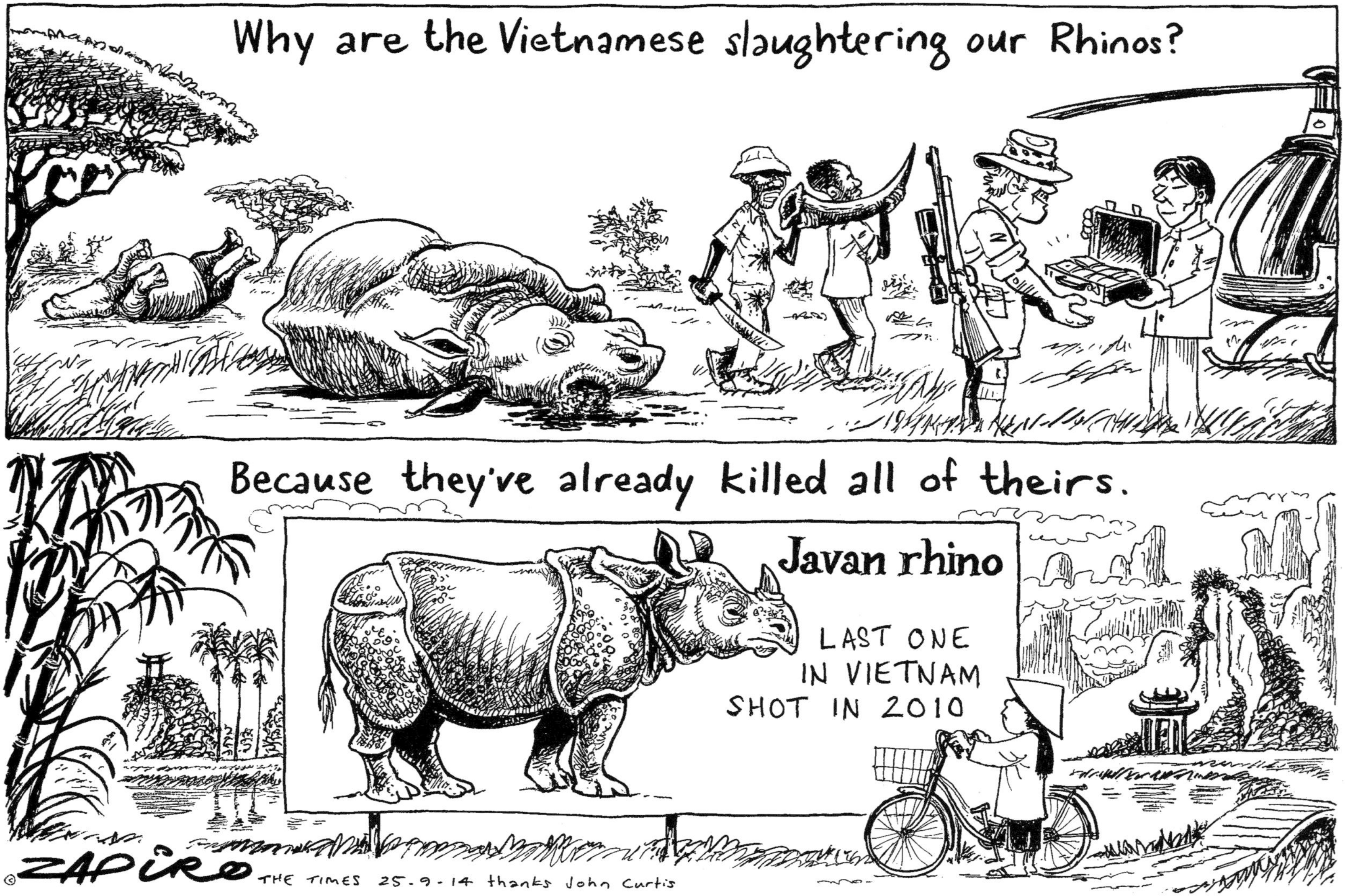
Why are the Vietnamese slaughtering our Rhinos?
Because they've already killed all of theirs.
Javan rhino
LAST ONE
IN VIETNAM
SHOT IN 2010
© ZAPIRO THE TIMES 25-9-14 thanks John Curtis

25 September 2014

21 September 2014

Baleka Mbete doesn't see a problem with being chairperson of the ANC while presiding over parliament and neither does her party, who kill off a no-confidence motion against her

1 October 2014

The DA's Mmusi Maimane calls parliament's ad hoc committee on Nkandla 'Operation Protect Zuma at All Costs' and leads a walk-out

Sunday Times reports Zuma accepted a bribe from a French arms company in 2000 by using the code words 'I see the Eiffel Tower lights are shining today'

5 October 2014

Planned Nobel Peace Laureate Summit in Cape Town to honour Madiba is boycotted by foreign Peace Prize winners protesting SA government's treatment of the Dalai Lama